The Footloose Gardener.
By Neil Timm

Published in the United Kingdom
by R. N. Timm, The Fern Nursery.

Published 2018

ISBN 978-1-5272-1967-0

Introduction

It is in the nature of all gardeners no matter where they come from to tell stories, and here you will find no more than just such a ragbag of tales, gleaned from beneath a nearby gooseberry bush, that many an old grey beard with a red nose could tell.

And if, as sometimes happens, when he is out working, your gardener straightens his back a little to look over the fence at the even wilder world beyond, then you should forgive him, since these are not in any way intended as just practical works. It is no good looking anywhere here if you wish to find out how to set the blades on your lawn mower, or how deep to plant your seeds. In fact if you are yourself already enough of a pragmatist to find all the joy that you need in doing such things, then you do not really need to read any more of this.

Since informing all these bits of work is just one central idea, the 'big idea' if you like. Which is simply that, the greater our skill in the art of appreciation, then the less we shall be forced to rob from the world to fill our proper desires and needs, and that appreciation is best cultivated like everything else in a garden. This never was, I think, a bad idea, even in my youth when the word 'Green' was just the colour of grass.

Contents

Chicory

In my youth we lived down on the lowlands in Lincolnshire's central vale, the so-called 'Clay Vale', where the soil is heavy, sad, cold, and immovable with spade, fork or even plough as the name suggests. It was then quite a pleasure in many ways as a gardener to move up into a high Wolds valley where the soil is a few feet of light loam over a bed of free draining chalk.
Gardeners on really heavy clay often make a joke that, clay is just as easy to move with a spade or fork and just as easy to draw a hoe through, as any other soil, 'but only for one week in spring and one week in autumn.' The point of the joke is that in winter the wet and cold turn the clay into a kind of heavy sodden pudding that clings to and sucks at your tools so that they often go 'pop', like a jam jar lid as you break the vacuum and let the air in; while in summer it bakes hard, like crude pottery, and you would struggle to mark your soil with a sharp knife, let alone dig it. Some people will smile at this description because sadly it's only gardeners who really know, and especially those have worked with clay of the heaviest sort, who will realise that neither of those statements are in any way exaggerated.
The other pleasure of moving was the experience of living with a whole new range of wild plants and animals. True, the cow parsley doesn't grow as tall and lush here, nor is the garden as frequently enlivened by a lithe and glossy green grass snake, streaking through the deep green grass, which in the vale was often still moist on even the hottest of summer days. The ground here is certainly dryer and less fertile, much harder on things that revel in luxury and rich living but the higher thinner ground is brightened with many delicate flowers and herbs – hawkweed, harebells and thyme, for example – unique to the chalk Wolds which more than compensate for any losses. The wild chicory especially, is completely absent from my part of the lowlands but up here it is a common feature of the hedgerows, making a grand show in June, with its bright sky blue, daisy-type flowers, two or more inches across, on top of long, waist-high stems.

**

One particularly impressive clump grows on the roadside verge near a little crossroads, high up on top of the Wolds, where two minor lanes meet, a place I pass regularly on my walks. I always enjoy the

chicory there, partly because its large blue flowers are almost, but not quite, untainted with any touch of violet. A perfect blue, which is such a rare colour in our wild flowers that it is always to be admired at any time but up in the wide open sky spaces of the high Wolds, looking up at the equally blue sky, it seems extra special.
One day, when out walking with a representative of both a more sensitive species and a wiser gender, I had to stand beside the chicory for some time while she investigated some rabbit runs, (which apparently takes quite a long time to do properly). And being forced to wait until she was finished, I began to wonder why no one ever uses wild chicory as a garden plant, it being so refined in appearance and perfect in colour. I had an idea that it could be a little invasive, but what wild flower is not? Usually I'm undaunted by vigour in a plant, since controlling even the very aggressive is far better than going to a gymnasium for your health, while a little squirt of weedkiller always works if I'm feeling lazy, and I have quite a rough garden with a number of wild corners so there's little concern for neatness. Fortunately the chicory grew as a weed in a neighbour's hedge, so a small piece was easily domesticated into a border just behind the house.

It then did little more than sit there without moving or flowering through all of the first summer, and in the winter it died away so completely that at first glance it looked as though I'd lost it. Which didn't come as a great surprise since most gardeners know from experience that the wildest and toughest of wild weeds can often, paradoxically, be the most difficult to cultivate in the gentle and more sheltered setting of a garden.
However it wasn't dead at all, and the following spring it returned in quantity. It had obviously not been anything like as inactive as it seemed that first summer but had been steadily and persistently pushing its way forward beneath the ground because little plants began to spring up almost everywhere, even at a distance of several feet from the original plant. It had spread down among the roots of the herbaceous perennials and had infiltrated its way into even the most difficult and inaccessible corners where no fork or spade could ever hope to remove it.
I remember once many years ago a gardener of great experience pouring scorn on people who confessed to being afraid of any so-called 'invasive' plants. "Have they forgotten how to use the spade and the hoe?" he asked. Very true – why should any gardener

be scared to grow any plant just because of its possible vigour, and surely only requiring some work in the garden to keep things under control? But it's just possible that my friend's experience was limited, and that he had never encountered some of nature's most vigorous plants.

There is, after all, as in most things, a balance of economy in this. The plant's beauty and interest which earns it a place in the garden must be balanced against both the beauty and interest of the other plants which would otherwise occupy its space, also the stress caused to other plants by digging and pulling, and the relative work needed by the gardener.

However, I decided not to panic and did nothing with the chicory immediately, so that in the second summer that part of the border was filled with the most lovely blue flowers waving in the wind, and looking glorious, delicate and exotic. So much so, that it attracted many admiring comments from even quite blasé garden visitors. Until that is, the flowering was finished when the plants were immediately cut down before they could seed, and then the rosettes of leaves were sprayed thoroughly with a strong systemic weedkiller, carefully covering all the chicory leaves but avoiding those of the other plants. It seemed a poor way to treat it but it was not the only plant I had to consider – the border was not exclusive to the chicory. A couple of follow-up visits to the border later in the year ensured it was really gone, and it has not – perhaps regrettably – returned since. I am now fairly confident it has gone forever, but was it worth the experiment? Indeed it was.

Frost

The winter of 2010/11 was perhaps the coldest and snowiest of the last two decades and we saw things happening that many younger people can hardly recall. To a lot of people in Britain it must have been a great novelty, and certainly the first encounter for most of those under twenty-five with that quite rare phenomena which their more pompous elders would call a 'proper British winter'. For the first time in years icicles as thick as your arm were seen hanging from gutters, and frost ferns appeared on the inside of windows. Both of which must have been quite new to many. Even for those whose memories do go back a little, there were a number of surprises both magical and shocking.

One thing rarely seen in on this windy isle was the way in which the snow fell day after day without any wind or consequent drifting. Here on the top of the Wolds where we caught quite a lot of snow, it eventually formed an even, heavy blanket over everything, reaching halfway up the thighs of people brave enough to go walking out. It covered the ground level vegetation completely, making it difficult for the smaller herbivores which still needed their regular supplies of green stuff. How they solved their problem soon began to show on the grass verges and in the meadows immediately after the thaw. You only needed to look down at the ground and it was hard to miss the runs made by the really tiny herbivores as they moved around their small worlds. The runs showed up quite plainly as they would normally never do on the surface of the grass – my guess would be that the voles and other small creatures had continued to use their normal trackways as tunnels under the snow, but the heavy use of those tunnels, perhaps accompanied by extra heavy grazing near the sides of them, resulted in these clear grooves in the grass. That is, of course, merely wild speculation on my part as there could be other reasons for the passages but I'm sufficiently confident about it to let it pass for knowledge until someone proves me wrong.

There was also plain evidence of the struggle for survival by rabbits in the hedgerows. Walking along some of the more rabbit-haunted lanes, you could easily see that the bark on the hedgerow shrubs had been heavily gnawed just above the snow line. In many cases the bark had been completely removed all round the trunks in a strip between two and three feet above the ground. I surmised that the hedge would die back in the spring, because the shrubs had suffered a fatal blow but remember pondering on what the replacement growth would be like. I tried to work out if there was any evidence of this happening in previous years. I monitored what happened and unfortunately in spring, the hedge did indeed die back.

Perhaps the biggest shock of that winter was the early onset of the cold weather and snow coming before November was out, and in its first incarnation, lasting for several weeks without respite. I think it was that factor of persistence, perhaps more than anything, which did the damage in the gardens. Many plants will, I suspect, withstand just one night of frost quite happily even if it's very sharp, because a daily thaw limits the depth of its penetration. A frost, however, that lasts through the daylight hours and continues to add, however little, to the freezing depth for a whole day or more on end is, from a plant's point of view a different matter entirely; and in 2010/11 the frost was continuous, not just for days but for weeks. When that happens, the depth to which the icing reaches into the soil and into the plant's tissues continues to grow, getting deeper and deeper with every day. Eventually the soil freezes to the point where many of the plant's roots are no longer able to access water, and it is that above all which is really deadly, especially to evergreens which still need water for their leaves even in winter. The frost need not even be hard, it's the depth to which it reaches over time that proves the killer. Certainly this seems to be the case with the Cabbage Palms, Trachycarpus, which were considered hardy even in the early twentieth century, long before the recent run of mild winters. The last great winter of legend was 1916, and E J Salisbury wrote about it in in the 1930s, in his wonderful but not very PC book, The Living Garden. He considered it hardy even then and says that a mature plant is frost tolerant down to -30°. Our very old plants, however, did not live through the winter of which I write, even at only half that depth of frost, for this time it went on for days and froze the palms' trunks right through to the core. Frost remained even in the middle of the afternoon for weeks on end, something that I had not seen since the 1980s. Consequently the soil became frozen solid more than a foot below the surface, and it became impossible to dig a hole.

**

Some of those on the list of plants which failed in most of the gardens round here were hardly surprising, Pittisporums, the Shrubby Veronicas that were once known as Hebes; Penstemon, Phormium, Fatsia, Fushias, Summer Jasmine, Bay trees and Rhobinia were all cut down in our area. This is only to be expected, since most of these were traditionally on the informal list of plants which gardeners considered tender. That was especially so in my youth, when gardeners would shake their heads at the thought of planting any of them outside the greenhouse but a couple of decades of mild winters had conditioned gardeners to expect to get away with much more than they ever would have then. Hopefully the relative cheapness of plants today means that we are no longer quite so precious about them and will perhaps accept with more grace that they may only last a year or two.

Yet some other plants that were hit came as a complete surprise. Privet hedges which according to folklore are the very pinnacle of tough hardiness, were very badly browned, though scraping the bark of a neighbour's hedge revealed bright green below, so they hadn't died but merely turned deciduous. (Unfortunately, time proved that they were dead.) Many shrubs, however, usually regarded as quite hardy, such as Viburnum tinus and Mahonias were hammered badly, even if not quite killed. A large number of Beriberis darwiniae, for example, were badly scorched and some killed outright. Conifers too, such as the ultra-hardy Junipers but these were broken by snow rather than the frost, and I'm inclined to wonder if it might be the continual soft British seasons (which had proceeded this winter for many years, and which eventually led to overly large lush growth never seen in the plants' native lands) which was in fact at fault. Rosemary and lavender, however, the two grey-leaved Mediterranean shrubs, often thought to be dubious if not quite risky, both passed through well. Could it be as some people say, that their fragrant oils act as a form of antifreeze? Certainly garden lore holds that it is damp rather than cold which makes them vulnerable in British winters. And, as always with these things, it's important to remember that these two weather phenomena are quite capable of working together in combination – either at the same time or in repeated succession – and can do the harm that one alone couldn't accomplish. Sometimes you may hit just a once in a hundred year combination of weathers that knocks some normally hardy plants one way then the other, so that they fall down beneath a combination of punches, and can't rise again. As always in the garden, there are more questions still to be answered.

Primrose

Snowdrops flower and pass slowly away, the change from one day to the next hardly noticeable, for as with all winter flowers in the cold stiff season they must take time and wait for the few pollinators that are available; they also hang their flowers downwards to protect the vital organs within from the weather as long as possible. As do the hellebores, only starting to lift their tough enduring heads higher as their season draws to an end. But by then the season is ready for the primroses, the Primula, to flower, as perhaps the first of the true spring flowers with truly upturned blooms, just when we begin to see the last of the winter blooms going over. Yet the over-familiar often passes without notice or remark, so that I find people are often surprised when I point out to them the seemingly obvious derivation of the word primrose, which is truly the 'prime rose', the first rose of the year. It can only be because the name and the plant are so widely used and seen which causes this, since everyone to whom I have ever pointed it out always says, "Of course," in that way which means, "how silly, I should have spotted that".

In fact, as you well know I'm sure, the primrose isn't really a rose at all, nor even a close relative – cyclamen would be a better choice – but you can see a slight resemblance in the open flowers to a single yellow rose, and no doubt wishful thinking during the bleak days of late winter for the beginning of the rose season, made the poetic connection almost inevitable. Yet I think that if you really need a rose to cheer you in the spring, then you've missed something quite special, since surely there could be no flower better suited to warm your spirits on a bleak day than a wild primrose. Often the one bright star of green and yellow nestled in the bottom of the still dormant and winter-blasted hedgerows seems so cheerful as to be almost unnatural.

Take a closer look if you will, and you'll see the blossom isn't merely yellow but a whole symphony of rich butter tones, from gold through lemon green to almost white, yet not one of the delicate tints is ever dull or cold. Could there be a better reminder of life's vigour and resilience than the almost tissue thin bloom which the primrose unfolds in what is very often the harshest of seasons?

The Japanese build a whole mythology and set festivals around their cherry blossom for just that reason, and yet the primrose is much brighter and more vulnerable in its blossom and being a small herb, far more in contrast with the season's climate when it flowers than a large woody tree. Yet at this end of the northern hemisphere our own gentle Amazon of the snows is passed almost unnoticed, let alone with a festival to its name.

What's more, there are so many other things that the primrose has to offer which makes its humble, disregarded status doubly sad. For one thing there is a whole range of cultivated forms derived from the primrose family, with every form of double flowers, frilled and cut petals you could wish for, and with petals in every colour of the rainbow, including blue and green. Just think of the fanfare that awaits anyone who could breed a true blue rose, yet to the best of my knowledge the Primulas have not even a single good monograph in print to their name, though it has to be said that none of the coloured and fancy forms ever seem to me half as beautiful as the simple wilding seen in the hedgerow.

And I've also noticed that in primroses especially, the plants with flowers of unnatural colours never seem to have the surviving and growing vigour that the yellow cultivars, even the large flowered ones, seem to show. In this they aren't unique because many garden plants seem to show greater strength and vigour when grown in their natural coloured forms. It may well be that there's a natural economy at work in deciding the pigments that flowers produce, especially in the spring, and that producing other colours not intended by nature puts an extra strain on the plant. It's therefore perhaps no bad thing that the Primulas readily cross breed, and I find that in my garden the rainbow shades are gradually fading away, to be replaced with just the naturalised yellows, and perhaps a few reds which still linger annoyingly in their dullness, like boring bar-flies still hogging their stools long after closing time.

**

Let me persuade you take an even closer look at the flowers. Come on have a go – I promise a little botany will do you no harm. You'll find that the primrose would be far from dull even if it wasn't brightly coloured and it bloomed at the height of summer, because the flower is really quite sophisticated in structure. You'll not find, for example, any separate petals because they're all fused together into a trumpet-like tube, while the sepals protecting them in the bud stage are almost the same, and even the male stamens which carry the pollen aren't truly separate but emerge from the sides of the tube part way up – quite a neat, efficient plan if you think about it. For though it's true that the primrose is a fairly simple flower, not a supposedly advanced compound flower like the daisies, or richly complex like many an orchid or a pea flower with lots of petals, all of which have different functions; yet I think this plain economy deserves some respect because the primrose's simple tube is about as supple as it is possible for evolution to make the design of an open flower which has only equal and symmetrical parts, and nothing more.

It is quite profound in the economic styling of its structure, with a sort of minimalist streamlined efficiency of every part and nothing redundant, something often admired in the human arts – and a refinement that would surely win it prizes if it were designed by a structural engineer and was not a simple wayside flower.

But the wonders of the primrose don't end there, because there's another real stroke of genius built into the flower's design that impresses me even more, and I hope will impress you too. It is this: the primrose has found a very straightforward but effective way of preventing its own seeds from being self-fertilised by its own pollen, a device that can even reduce the chances of being pollinated by its close relatives, yet without any of the elaborate mechanisms for the same purpose we see in some flowers such as orchids.

Quite simply the flowers on primroses all come in one of two variations called 'pin-eye', where the female stigma shows at the top near the opening of the flower, and 'thrum-eye', where it is hidden deep down, while the male stamens attached to the sides of the flower tube follow the opposite rule in each flower. So this means that plants with the short female stigma have stamens which only place their pollen on a visiting insect high up near the rear end of its tongue or body, where it can't be reached by the short stigma, while those with long stigmas place their stamens and pollen on the tip of the insect, deep inside the flower, which is then swiftly withdrawn past the tall stigma before it can shed much pollen.

Consequently, a thrum-eyed primrose may only fertilise a pin-eyed and visa-versa. In this way the Primula and several of its relatives endeavour to avoid any form of accidental incest. This may well be an especially good strategy for spring flowering plants which enjoy a very few warm days when the insects are active, and therefore need to have both their male and female sexual organs active at the same time, unlike the summer flowers which may enjoy more leisured courtships.

Strangely the different forms – thrum and pin – taken by the primrose flowers have been known to folklore, and especially children's lore for centuries. It often seems truly amazing the detail that perfectly ordinary people in the Middle Ages observed in the natural world and thought worthy of passing on. Yet we humans in the past seemed to have been so poor at drawing any insights from those observations; it was not until Charles Darwin pointed it out in the middle of the nineteenth century, that anyone realised the purpose the duality served. In fact within Darwin's own lifetime little more than two hundred years ago, there still lived people who called themselves natural philosophers, who yet didn't believe that plants had sex lives at all, and debated the point with venom. This is despite the fact that as one of the earliest of green poets, Donald C Peattie, pointed out, people had by then been raising both daughters and fruit trees for thousands of years, and had patiently watched both grow to maturity until they bore fruit, yet still the penny didn't drop.

So sometimes I feel that it's a nice conceit to keep up an old custom now and again, just like that of looking into a primrose flower to see if it's a pin or a thrum eye. In fact I may even extend the idea this spring and try to count and see what the balance of types are in my garden, and the hedgerows round the village. It seems like a pleasant and harmless enough pastime that might amuse anyone not allergic to the countryside. And that little act of reverence to nature will put you at the same time into one spirit with the innocence of medieval children playing betting and counting games in the copse and dell, that is when the harsh necessity of the age spared them. And at the same time with the deep wisdom of the old white bearded Darwin, plodding his aged mile or two round the sand walk at the bottom of his garden, and dreaming of a new Galapagos from an English country field.

Trade

I have the great good fortune to have employed myself for many years now, in a form of business that used to be termed 'trade'. I hope that this article will explain why I think that fact seems worthy of writing about, because sadly it's not usual today to see 'trade' as anything more than a way of making a living. Yet it is I think quite an unfortunate thing for people of any age to develop that attitude, since just making a living is far from being the best thing about the simple direct business of retail selling, and it certainly doesn't begin to compare with the huge amount of quiet joy which trading brings in its own right. It could well be one of the saddest signs of just how cynical our world has become that pleasure and shared joy are not always the first things that the venerable word, 'trade' brings to mind. Parts of my business concern trade in the most basic sense of the word, operating sometimes from something akin to a market stall, which is perhaps about as close to the fundamental origins of retailing in its original and ancient form as you can achieve today – and maybe it's this very basic and simple form of my trade that makes it such a joy. And trading in living plants is itself especially satisfying, being able to set up my stall at a wonderfully wide range of venues, from city centre markets and grand buildings to some of the most beautiful gardens imaginable, the wide range of geographic experiences helping to add to the pleasure.

**

Yet it's the social pleasures that stand out the most. Even if the business and the day's takings are slow, the trader, snugly installed behind the market stall, still has an unequalled opportunity for watching people. The stall becomes a kind of hide from which the careful watcher can observe what is arguably the most fascinating of all animals. People-watching is of course at its best on a warm summer's day which, with its promise of shopping, garden visiting, picnicking and grass for the children to romp on, brings out nearly the whole human race at its liveliest.

There are families with children, circling, chattering and squabbling like flocks of noisy sparrows; father and mother, whose banter between the flowers is perhaps far more good natured than it ever is anywhere else, debating quietly what plant is best for where and who shall push the pram while the other is freed to follow their own special interests. Though in fact pushing the baby's transport is no great hardship, since public gardens are perhaps one of the few places where the pleasure of pushing a pram still lives up to its promise.

These customers always buy their plants in a mood of trepidation because it would be a shame to miss the chance of buying a hard-to-find treasure when it's right in front of them. Yet they know that if they buy it, then it must be carefully defended against the rough play of children, along with their equally boisterous animal accomplices, for perhaps many years before the plant will have a chance to really fulfill its potential. Will it therefore be a waste of money? Will it die? Should we wait till they're older? Yet we've wanted it for so long, and here it sits asking for a home?

Sometimes the public can be unkind and you overhear comments such as the, "I really hate those – they're just weeds to me," made by two women who walked past my stall at one fair. But these things are rare.

Not so with the newly wedded or soon-to-be wedded couple; they're eager and filled with enthusiasm for planting up what is perhaps their first garden. In the warm sun and the holiday mood of the day, they're keen to indulge each other and bask in the warmth of mutual patronage, so that in the end he often buys her plants, and she buys his. And all the while both are trying hard to impress the other with the depth of their appreciation, academic knowledge and domestic wisdom, proudly announcing some minor scrap of botanic trivia as proof of a commitment to higher things. And if sometimes the stallholder should overhear a statement of wild inaccuracy being uttered in tones of great authority... well, as long as no plant will suffer by it, it seems best just to smile and nod.

The keenest of the lone males are generally the collectors, earnestly in search of plants to fill the gaps in their collections. They root thoroughly through the stock you have on display as though hunting for buried treasure, though (being male and brash!) they nearly always miss the one thing they most seek. Then when at last they ask you for it by name, they look completely surprised when you point out that it's one of the things they stepped over on their way to the stall.

The most earnest of women on the other hand are always those on the cusp of maturity, eager for new adventures now that their children have flown, and they have both the time and a garden to themselves at last. They tour the garden in costumes of bright

summer colours, trailing long trains of bags and baskets. Keen perhaps to make their gardens flower all the more, as they begin to feel – quite wrongly of course – that their own bloom is fading.
The yet older ladies have regained their composure and seem in many ways to be the best and most competent of buyers. I must be honest here, though, and say that their kindliness in sharing the fruits of their wisdom and experience with younger persons is sometimes seasoned with just a faint savour of half-concealed vanity, "Oh, you don't want that. The old pink flowered form is much more robust, take my word for it!"

When I was a lot younger, the best of these ladies still carried lists of wanted plants all written out neatly in careful longhand, and often in recycled diaries – habits of thrift and discipline which they no doubt formed in more formal and better organised days than now, when plants and notebooks were expensive luxuries, and trips in cars to nurseries rare treats.
But sadly these well organised lists are now seen much less often with every passing year, and for younger people plant buying is becoming a lot more casual and spur of the moment; perhaps that is no bad thing. Yet it was fun and enlightening to read the lists which were often proffered for you to read yourself, with the question, "Have you any of those?" Especially when you have nearly all of 'those' and you can witness a look of surprise and delight on the face of your customer. (Often followed by an "Oh dear," and a hasty rummage through the purse!)
It may not be quite all over yet, though, because I've recently noticed that some of the younger gardeners have now started to carry lists written into phones and pocket computers, so maybe there's hope for the future of plant collecting as a hobby after all.

**

One thing I've learned over the years is that for every plant there is a buyer, no matter how humble or plain that plant might be. I remember one plant fair many years ago, taking along my then girlfriend for company and the pleasure of a sunny day out. That same day I also took a small plant, the small horsetail Equisetum scirpoides. Now not even the best Equisetum in the world could ever be described as a front runner among popular plants, and E. scirpoides is not an impressive plant at the best of times, being just a little green rush-like thing that likes to grow near water, and rarely reaches knee high. This one, however, was especially modest because it was newly grown and just a little tuft of green in a small pot.

Normally I wouldn't have taken a plant so small to a fair but it was new to my list and I was eager to offer it for the first time. Helping me unpack, my girlfriend lifted it out of the box and peered at it with curiosity and disdain, "Whatever have you brought that for, nobody will ever buy it. It just looks like a tuft of grass." However it went on the table and sat there looking sad for some ten minutes or so. Then a middle-aged man approached the table, and glancing along the plants, immediately picked up the Equisetum. "Marvellous! I've been looking everywhere for that," he said, and bought it quickly before asking if I had any more. I gave my girlfriend my warmest beam.

Not that you can succeed every time, or that it will be every day that brings lots of chances to help enhance some gardener's life. There are, quite naturally, the dismal days when the rain falls and there are no customers to speak of. Yet even on these days there are still some joys, for it's rare that you won't take enough money to cover your expenses, and if you're relaxed with this, then you may be content. It is, after all, no bad profession which will let you sit in a garden beneath an umbrella with a cup of tea, watching the refreshing rain fall and exchanging gossip with your competitors.

But always, whoever or how few the customers are, there's the satisfaction to be had in bringing along and selling something that someone really needs or is in some way delighted with, which makes all your efforts seem worthwhile. Trade seems to be a natural thing to humans, something that grows everywhere out of the fundamental nature of our biology – an 'emergence' as science would call it, and what a wonderful thing it is. That the natural competitiveness all animals share should, in one species at least, be almost completely subverted into helping others to enhance their lives; this is a truly great and wonderful new departure for life if ever there was one. How therefore can it be said that trade is not a thing of deep worth, as enhancing to the spirit as communing with nature or meditation?

Butterfly

Today I went to see a collection of tropical butterflies housed in a large greenhouse, at a so-called 'Butterfly Farm'. At first it didn't seem too interesting since reaching the butterfly house meant passing through the inevitably bland gift shop. Eventually however I found the modest door hidden away at the back that led to what the owners clearly regarded as the less important part of the venue. But however uninspiring the introduction, it could not distract from the delight of the main exhibit. In fact, having entered the greenhouse, I found wandering round the winding paths, between dense planting of flowering shrubs, in an atmosphere of gentle Mediterranean warmth, while watching the fluttering antics of the many butterflies, a pleasant and relaxing way to pass the time. It's more than possible to lose yourself for a long while in the company of the Lepidoptera. What impressed me most, apart from the sheer numbers to be seen in such a small space, was the spectacular size of many tropical species. Impressive too was the way that some of the larger species seem to fly – in a manner, and with a rhythm of wing beats much more like that of birds, than is usual with our own temperate British butterflies.

After a half hour or so spent walking round admiring these magnificent tropical insects going about their daily routine, I sat down quietly to continue watching them. While I sat, I was reminded of summer days in my own garden where I can stand by a large Buddleia bush and watch our native butterflies feeding. On the best days, the abundance around this bush far exceeds in numbers the display to be seen gathered on any one spot in the elaborate, expensive and extravagantly heated tropical house.

There is a territorial law at work with pollinating insects, perhaps involving the rate at which plants can yield nectar, which limits the numbers of butterflies visiting any one plant at any one time. Certainly based on what I saw that day, the butterflies in the greenhouse seem to have a habit of spreading themselves fairly evenly. Whatever it is, the same rules of distribution may well apply in both garden and greenhouse (though don't quote me on this). And this they do greatly to my garden's credit, since a lot of trouble and expense has gone into creating the farms display, while the buddleia only cost me a pound or two, and half an hour's work every now and then.

But an even richer thought then came to me that, however large and impressive the tropical species may be, I'm not convinced any of them are any better coloured than our own natives. Certainly none is any brighter in colour than our own common garden Red Admiral. While there are few which, however ornate and sophisticated their design, manage to excel the gentle Tortoiseshell for its subtlety of painting. And for pure style and panache of colouring, the best of them can only really hope to equal that of the native Yellow Brimstone, or the Small Blue which you may see by almost any untrimmed hedge side in any good British summer. So I left the venue with an unexpected feeling of gentle national pride in the natural history and life of my own country – certainly one of the last things that I had expected as I passed through the unprepossessing gift shop.

Glass

The winter of 2010 was quite exceptional, we had snow up here on the Wolds which fell heavily and straight downwards for day after day, with no hint of the usual mid-winter winds or drifting at all, until the snow reached a depth of more than two feet thick. In doing so, it created a serious problem for all those with greenhouses, whether of polythene bubble like ours, or the more conventional type of framed glass. Normally during most British winters it's the drifting of snow that's seen as the major problem, filling in the roads and blocking paths as it does, even when there's only been a light dusting overall, but at least the drifting keeps the snow off the roofs to some extent. However this time it just fell as a solid dead weight on to any flat or nearly flat surface it could find – so much so that we were forced to go out repeatedly in the coldest weather, equipped with brooms attached to the ends of long poles, to sweep the vulnerable greenhouses clear of the pressure that threatened to crush them. Eventually even the snow we swept off became a problem in its own right, piled four or five feet deep between the greenhouses. It became so difficult to move, between some of the polythene tunnels especially, that I was forced to wear waist-high waders just to force a way through. Had there been one more snowfall we might have been defeated because there was simply nowhere else left to put the snow, but fortunately for us, after reaching a depth of perhaps two feet, it stopped just in time.

Consequently we didn't lose any of our structures to the snow. Maybe we did enough, or maybe we were just lucky because when the thaw came and we began to venture out and rejoin the local social round of nurseries and garden centres, we soon discovered that many of our friends had fared far worse. All across the county we heard tales of people losing acres of glasshouses and most of the wintering crops within them.

When things like this happen, it's not just the material cost of losing cover that matters most to the grower, because I don't know of a person in the whole industry for whom greenhouses, and the life lived within them, are not the subject of at least some affection and pride – second only perhaps to that which they have for their homes. There are maybe as many reasons for becoming a grower as there are growers but I'm sure that the more common considerations for many of them when they choose their career must be the pleasure and the challenge that the greenhouse and the cultivation within it give. In the greenhouse the grower can try their hand at playing God, growing plants not usually seen at all in their outdoor climate, propagating seedlings and cuttings too tender to survive outside, and changing the seasons to suit themselves and the whims of their customers. The grower can step into the house from the winter cold and see fresh green shoots carpet the ground when all the natural world outside is dead and brown. This is something approaching the sort of pleasure and satisfaction that I should think is enjoyed by those who irrigate the desert, creating a lush oasis from a little trickle of water, hard won by wit and long labour from the distant mountains' rocky seepage.

**

But for me at least I think that the greatest pleasure of the greenhouse by far is the rich vein of associations that entry into a greenhouse unleashes in my mind. Some of my earliest memories come with glasshouses attached. To children they are always wonderlands, set apart as they are from the rest of the everyday world in much the same mysterious way that the fairylands of literature are. Yet even in the deep cynicism of high youth, some of my most vivid memories were formed under glass.
Memories such as the old greenhouse I knew at horticultural college. Wooden framed and brick walled, it must have been a considerable investment when it was built in some distant time long ago when even the ancient college was young. But by the seventies it was looking hopelessly out of date and far too small to be a practical building, even just to demonstrate the bare principles of modern commerce; by my day it had become a spare house, used for nothing more than to store stock plants for identification tests. This, however, helped in many ways to make it seem a special place, since it was full to the brim with diversity and interest, fragrant and warm even in the coldest weather, generally neglected by passers-by and mellowed by time. Its crumbling brick paths and wild moss gardens beneath the benches made it the perfect place to sneak into for quiet solitary study, reading and scribbling in the dry warm air while summer rain pattered outside.

Shortly after I left, however, it met the natural fate of all old things and was inevitably pulled down. In order to make way for – well, who really cares what shiny new aluminium gadget? If it were still standing today in the new age of conservation it would probably be a listed building, but back then in the sixties and seventies, knocking old things down was all the fashion. But please don't misunderstand – for myself, while I'm sad sometimes to see things let go or pulled down that I have a personal affection for, I can't love the heritage industry. Attempting to make the country into a museum seems to be a deviant pursuit for a nation that can't be bothered even to teach its children history, from which they can learn real universal truths. No, change that word 'deviant' because for a country to throw out the true lessons of history, to preserve a twee sentimental past is, in fact, 'stomach churningly deviant'. But real history that stretches the mind in exactly the same way that travel is conventionally said to do, taking the imagination into other lands that are so foreign even the disembodied mind sometimes struggles to find its passport and visas – that is a treasure beyond price.

**

Growing plants outside of their natural seasons, soils or climates was always a highly desirable thing to do in any age but it must have been especially so in the very distant past, especially before the Industrial Revolution when the products of growing things made up a much greater part of people's resources. Yet surprisingly, despite that, there seems to be little evidence that anyone much before the Romans, around the first century BC, practiced any form of environmental control for plants excepting, that is, for simple irrigation borrowed from farming practices, and of course the provision of walls and fences. These latter were usually said in historical literature to be there to keep the wildlife at bay, although I suspect it was probably mainly human wildlife and domestic stock which were targeted by these fortifications.
Despite that, even the provision of a walled enclosure, such as those found in ancient Egypt and Mesopotamia, which for a long time was the main feature which defined the garden as something different from farming, shows what a truly high value was placed on the plants within. Yet there doesn't seem to be any early record of attempts made to provide special environments for exotic plants from distant places, or of any attempt to force plants out of season. I suspect that the earliest faltering steps in that direction have simply escaped the records. It could well be, however, that when exotic plants were very rare indeed and there was only limited knowledge

about their care, then the odd spasmodic imports that must have occurred in most countries were not frequent enough for early cultures to build up an established body of knowledge about their care. So that when the strange foreign plants died, as they no doubt often did, then people just gave a xenophobic shrug of the shoulders and didn't bother to pass on the little they'd learned. Or maybe the wealthy garden owners simply had their gardeners' heads chopped off when the precious trees died, which pretty well put an end to the passage of experience.

**

With the Romans, however, the whole nature of gardening seems to change completely. By the time of their empire the world must have been sufficiently well connected up and communications so well formed that exotic plants were appearing regularly in trade, and there was by then a small but significant class of persons who had travelled widely enough to know their value. It therefore became possible for at least a small number of professional gardeners to begin building up a significant body of practical experience and knowledge about the cultivation of exotics. And there was also a large enough demand from the public for luxury goods of all sorts to support the forcing of produce out of season. Roses, it seems, were especially treated this way, perhaps because of their religious significance.

By Roman times, exotic plants and out-of-season crops were widely grown, and to make all this possible, special housing was certainly being built for tender and forced plants. Some of these structures were undoubtedly true greenhouses, since we are told in Roman literature they had windows which were glazed with sheets of mica, talc and other transparent minerals, though it seems these structures rarely extended beyond the gardens of the very wealthy. It would appear that even at the height of the empire, the most important technique used was simply to keep the plants in pots, lifting them out in the morning and back in again at night. There's no doubt that this intensive care has a lot to do with the availability of cheap slave labour but it almost certainly also represents the high relative value of plants and their products that existed in an age when, for example, a small melon field could form a large part of a soldier's pension provision.

What seems really strange about Roman greenhouses, however, is that they don't seem to have used glass for their windows, resorting only to natural mineral sheeting. Even more odd is, that of all cultures in the ancient world, few made so much glass or glassware of such quality as the Romans. Their decorative glassware was highly sophisticated, refined and technically advanced, and was produced in quite large quantities. It could be that despite the existence of the large glass industry, sheets of talc and mica were still cheaper to make, or it maybe that the idea of making glass into flat sheets and mounting them in frames to cover plants just never occurred to anyone. Yet despite the difficulties they had to overcome, Roman greenhouse culture was highly successful, to the extent that we are told the emperor Tiberius was able to serve fresh cucumbers, to which he was apparently addicted, on his table every day of the year.

**

Meanwhile at the other end of the old world in China, quite another style of greenhouse developed, based on windows glazed not with minerals but with translucent paper. These were not, however, merely expensive luxury buildings built by the wealthy for display, as much as for their produce.

In China there grew up a strong tradition of farmers and market gardeners using greenhouses for commerce. These were utility structures built of earth and the natural materials found to hand, with often the only cost being that of the paper itself. The paper was not, of course, weatherproof, and the structures had to be covered with straw-thatched frames at night or when storms threatened, but since parts of China enjoy long, cold, dry seasons this perhaps suited the climate fairly well, being at least no more labour intensive than the Roman habit of lifting the plants in and out. What the two contrasting styles of greenhouse culture really prove is just what a perfectly natural thing it is to want to protect growing plants, and how easily the habit grew up, quite independently, in totally different ways and in diverse parts of the world.

However, with the end of the Roman Empire, Europe lost its greenhouses and most of its other horticulture, a loss which lasted nearly a thousand years and, as you might guess, Europe only began to build a new greenhouse tradition with the Renaissance. It began slowly at first but as greater wealth spread through northern Europe in the late middle ages, so people began to grow exotic

plants. At first, no doubt, in small modest ways – perhaps just as pot plants in existing windows but from this there gradually grew the idea of making the window primarily for the plant, and then the building for the window, until the earliest records of real plant houses emerge in the early sixteenth century.
At first, of course, as with all things, the new technology was only available to the very rich, and usually used to produce luxury foods for the table. The Mediterranean diet extended steadily northwards through Europe where the well-known classical literature of Greece and Rome lent extra prestige to exotic plants such as lemons, pomegranates and grapes. The early plant houses were not always too successful – often in part due to taxes on glass, so frequently having nothing like enough glazing to supply the light needs of plants that came mostly from the sun brightened south. Consequently, the owners of the building were often forced to resort to the old Roman practice of lifting or wheeling the plants out on good days and putting them in at night. It was a long time before the names 'glasshouse' and 'greenhouse' entered the language, the buildings often taking their names from the plants grown in them, such as Orangery and Vinery, in order to gather a little of the prestige that goes with the exotic.

**

Protected growing really gathered speed in the late eighteenth and early nineteenth centuries. One after another, a whole series of technical and social developments came hurrying in, each pushing forward the culture of protected growing. The first came in the eighteenth century with the era of high farming, when farming reached the peak of fashion and became for the first time a true science in the enlightenment tradition. It naturally followed that if farming could be improved by the advance of science and technology, then so could gardening. And by 1800 walled enclosures filled with all manner of hotbeds heated by composting manure appeared, cloches and frames covered vast areas of terraces, sloped southward to catch the best of the sun, while wall hanging frames were sprouting everywhere, many of them having a modern feel with their skillful use of solar energy.
All the while the introduction of new plants was fuelling the demand for spaces to grow exotics. The large number of gardeners needed to maintain the fashionable kitchen gardens of the rich helped to

disseminate the demand, as well as the skills needed, through the wider community. Then in 1829 another development took place that at first must have seemed minor and peripheral but which almost certainly helped to stimulate the culture even more.

In that year a doctor called Nathaniel Ward made an important and original discovery. According to the tale that has been told many times but which well deserves repeating, Dr Ward was an enthusiastic amateur naturalist who had repeatedly tried to grow ferns and other delicate plants. He'd had little success though, mainly because his medical practice forced him to live in the depths of a smoke-laden industrial town where, thanks to the smog and its effect on people, he wasn't short of ailing patients but neither could any but the toughest plants live and thrive.

One day he put the chrysalis of a moth into a jar to hatch out, partially closing the mouth of the jar to prevent the moth escaping. He also put in some moist earth to prevent it becoming too dry, and placed it in semi-shade. The jar remained undisturbed for a long time, perhaps because the moth failed to hatch. However, many weeks later he found that a couple of plants had grown in the soil. One of the plants was a common grass but the other was a fern, which was just the kind of plant that he'd been trying to grow, without success, for a long time. He then realised that life in the closed jar had protected the fern from the worst effects of the air pollution, while not excluding anything that the plant needed such as sunlight, warmth and carbon dioxide. Moreover, the water in the soil condensing in the jar had been recycled to keep the plant moist without the need for any extra watering in several months.

This seemed like a good way to grow plants. It required very little care, not even watering and it seemed an especially easy way to grow difficult plants that wouldn't grow outside or in the normal home atmosphere. Dr Ward soon enlarged on his simple jar, making it into a large closed case with glass sides, and which the Victorians called a Wardian Case after its inventor, though today we more often call it a terrarium or bottle-garden. Wardian cases soon became very fashionable, enabling people to grow a whole range of plants never before seen in ordinary domestic homes and gardens, especially the exotic ones from places such as New Zealand, plants like the delicate filmy-ferns which require constant high humidity, warmth and a quiet, still air to grow at all.

So popular were the filmy-ferns as subjects for Wardian Cases that for a while they also acquired the popular name of Fern-Cases. It was soon found after a few simple experiments that Wardian Cases were ideal for transporting plants over long distances. Strapped to the decks of ships, the cases would protect living plants well, even from salt spray and the inattention of busy crews, enabling them to survive long sea voyages easily and in good health. This hugely increased the trade in exotic plants, and that in turn further fuelled the demand for the means to grow them.

However, the really important part played by the Wardian Case, from the point of view of the greenhouse story, was that it made people realise more than ever before that closed and semi-closed glass structures could be used to engineer artificial environments specially to suit plants needs. This soon led to the creation of the propagating frame, designed to keep cutting and seedlings moist until they could establish good roots, rapidly followed by the mist bench intended for the same purpose. Then came the alpine house, designed to keep killing damp and soot off fresh air loving mountain plants and even, to a degree, the water filled aquarium; all these following on naturally from the Wardian Case. Suddenly people realised that a few simple pieces of glass could open up whole ranges of the world's natural life, even to people who would never travel beyond their own parish boundaries.

**

All this led in the nineteenth century to an ever-growing cult of 'covered' growing. Soon greenhouses and conservatories were the height of fashion, and with the repeal of the punitive glass tax in 1845, many more people could afford the luxury of greenhouse culture. It all seemed very exciting to the education loving Victorian public because by simply growing a few exotic or tender plants, almost anyone of moderate means could feel that they were right at the cutting edge of science and fashion.

By the middle of the century the first great golden age of the glasshouse was well under way, not only in private gardens but in public spaces where huge, prestige structures were sprouting ever bigger and better. The most famous of these were probably William Caxton's great glass temples at Chatsworth, and most of all the Crystal Palace in London, which for a time was the largest building of any type in the world. But to my mind the greatest greenhouses of all were designed for Kew Gardens by Decimus Burton; they're much more accomplished aesthetically and happily they're still standing so you may admire them at first hand today.

Of the two, the Palm House is perhaps the more iconic, if only because it stands in a wonderful setting beside the great lake. However, without wishing to appear willfully obtuse, for me the Temperate House is by far the more interesting. Few structures could so completely express the age in which they were created as the Temperate House at Kew, sitting nestled among the trees like a fairytale wedding cake, with its three tiers taken apart and laid side by side on the floor of an equally enchanting fairy tale forest. The whole thing is encrusted with white sugar icing decorations of fanciful spires and leaf scrolls, all finely cast in iron and painted sparkling white. The space within invites you to drift slowly though a series of climate and geographical zones, an idea which many parks and gardens would consider bang up-to-the-minute, even in the twenty-first century.

And after admiring the Temperate House, you may move on to Kew's Water Lily House, the modern Alpine House, the traditional Orangery, or any one of several others all dating from different periods and made in different styles. And that's one of the great things that really sets Kew Gardens apart – the fact that it doesn't boast merely a large collection of greenhouses but a whole range of glasshouses from a series of periods in a great many styles. In effect, then, the whole garden becomes an architectural history lesson or an engineer's pattern book, making Kew well worth the visit for the greenhouses alone, even if it were not also an unsurpassed collection of plants.

The Victorian joy in sheltered cultivation simply grew and grew until no garden or civic park that considered itself a serious institution could be without a palm house or a winter garden, and even quite small borough councils could only keep up by budgeting for a hot house or two. The private gardens of the wealthy competed vigorously for the prestige of producing ever more and better exotic produce all year round to decorate the tables and windows of the great houses. And it is these, perhaps more than the public institutions, that spread the greenhouse culture throughout Victorian society until quite modest homes and the new allotments were familiar with at least the cold frame and the cloche, even though these were quite an investment for many people but the high price at least made sure they were skillfully and diligently used.

Even the famous Victorian craze for using vast numbers of bedding plants in gardens, (something that is often now derided as extravagant and outrageous), was really just a way of showing off the skills and technology of the greenhouse growers. We all know of course, the sad truth about what happened to the bedding fashion – a style so vibrant and extreme was bound to produce a reaction. So much so that people like William Robinson and Gertrude Jekyll today gain great credit for inventing the genteel cottage garden and promoting it as an antidote to the heavy and expensive Victorian bedding schemes, and although by so doing they had only an indirect effect on the glasshouses, the two world wars finished the job that they started, reinventing the greenhouse as purely, and perhaps a little puritanically, a practical tool for producing staple foods.

**

Yet I can remember that in my youth it was still possible, here and there in the old walled gardens, and in their sometimes crumbling, flaking and on occasions (but not often) lovingly restored greenhouses, to catch a last ghostly scent of the Victorian gentleman's freesia buttonhole, or see rows of old terracotta pots lined out on a traditional lime-washed wooden bench. Some of the old skills too just survived; there was still a tiny handful of people left in those days who could achieve the balances of soil moisture, air temperature and humidity by hand, skills which today modern growers rely on electronic metering and computers to achieve. Skilled ears could, for example, tell the water content of clay pots by 'ringing' them, as it was called, using a small wooden mallet made for the purpose.

Especially valued then was the condition known as a buoyant atmosphere. It's hard to describe what was meant by this but once you'd experienced it, you'd never forget it. It was achieved by careful use of heating, ventilation, watering and wetting down; the only way I can describe it best is almost the sort of air you get by the Mediterranean sea on warm evenings. Whether it was of as much benefit to the plants as was claimed I can't say but it certainly had a marked effect on human visitors. It was always tempting to run into the greenhouses just to breath in deeply the lightly fragrant air within.

As we all know, the greenhouse has begun a comeback in modern times. There's now a whole new range of materials and construction methods available so that they're no longer quite the luxury they once were, and most gardens of any worth need not be without one. Sadly that very cheapness – perhaps combined with the last shreds of the war time puritanism – probably accounts for the fact that few are ever used to their full potential, often being used for no more than a little propagating and storing of tools, as though they were merely well lit sheds.

It's true, of course, that when you create an improved environment for your plants you may also make a paradise for their pests and diseases, so that any form of greenhouse growing has always required a little more vigilance and expertise than gardening in the natural environment, which may put some people off – especially in this age of mindless technophobia and uninformed environmental dogma. Yet at the same time no one need depend on their small garden or allotment glasshouse today for sheer economic survival as many working class people did in the past; we can afford some losses, while great advances are made all the time in biological controls, so that we don't have to resort to the often frighteningly toxic poisons the Victorians used to keep their greenhouses healthy. At the same time, the professional glasshouse industry has never been more innovative than it is today, and whole realms of new technologies, methods of working and modes of construction are in use, some so advanced they couldn't even be envisioned less than half a century ago. And there are many signs of a revival in the public sphere, with a new generation of display houses built using new materials and designs and filled with exciting new exhibits, in places such as the Eden Project. Is it therefore perhaps too much to hope, even in this busy age when there are many distractions, that some of these ideas may begin to filter down through the whole of our culture, just as they did in Victorian times, and we may once again see the glasshouse as an important feature of the really happy home? That every village may have someone with a vine house, an alpine house, an orchid collection, or just a display of home produce a little more innovative than ten trusses of tomatoes.

Of course greenhouse culture as a pursuit for the keen amateur never disappeared entirely, even during two world wars. For though few people may grow oranges anymore, and the filmy-fern may be a mystery to most of us today, I know still an alpine grower or two, with rows of clay pots plunged into deep gravel beds on top of their benches, creating miniature scree-scapes of tiny green and flowered jewels. I also know an orchid grower with a household jungle, and a butterfly house filled with buddleias and other nectar yielding shrubs, while a whole tribe of bonsai growers bring their small works of art to show-bench perfection in a hundred back yard shelters. So that you may still get a greenhouse ‘fix’, if you need one as I do now and again. And perhaps now you know why I should be so very sorry if the snow were to flatten one of my tunnels.

The Heap

We all love a bonfire; even those of us old enough to imagine that we know better, and I generally find that the one thing that fades most with maturity, is your confidence in thinking you know better. A bonfire closes down so many of the garden's loose ends, and it livens the melancholy seasons of autumn and winter without ever truly injuring their gentle spirits, for what could chime with the mellow seasons more than a little woodsmoke and a small flame?

Sadly, however, the true garden bonfires are becoming ever rarer, and I suspect that a whole generation is growing up for whom the main association of fires is with something usually made with the sad remains of consumer products which were for the most part already rubbish before they left the shop. This is not what most of those who grew up in the rural traditions remember of, or want from, our garden fires but it is what may one day may make them more difficult and rare, if the environmental police get to know. And without being too environmentally precious, it's true that bonfires aren't always the most nature-friendly ways of using the garden's excess. Which of course, leaves you with two alternatives: put the stuff in the bin, which is perhaps even worse, or make a compost heap.

**

Composting is the 'PC' environmentally correct way of dealing with garden waste, which would normally make me reluctant to recommend it but fortunately I'm old enough, (just) to have known composting before the term 'politically correct' was a glimmer in a petty tyrant's eye, so I may recommend it with a clear conscience.

As I'm sure you know, the idea is to pile your waste into a corner or a bin and wait until the weather and the smaller members of the natural organic community, especially the fungi, have turned it into a soft brown mould which can be spread on the garden as a useful plant food and soil improver. The only requirements are a small amount of space in an unused corner of your plot, and a little patience.

This basic method is called cold composting and it works very well but as with most things, it can be improved upon if you're prepared to take a little more trouble, so for those who want a bit more of a challenge, there's a more refined method. This other method is called, naturally enough, "hot composting" and the main difference is that while cold compost is made by a whole range of creatures including insects, fungi, worms, woodlice and bacteria, hot compost is the product of just bacteria working almost alone.

The other difference is that it involves the gardener in a little more effort because hot compost needs to be 'turned' and it may also need watering, plus one or two other little acts of care and thought. However, the extra work involved is not great, and there is one huge and several small benefits. Which are that the hot heap kills the roots and seeds of weeds, plus any pests or diseases that may be present in the compost, much more completely, so it's safer to use and also gives you much better compost, and it does it a lot quicker.

**

Usually the hot compost starts out in much the same way as a cold heap, by simply piling up garden waste in some convenient place. It changes however when the pile gets to be big enough for you to bury a garden fork in without any of it sticking out. And with that lies the one real downside to hot compost because it's not therefore a method for the very small garden, since the main requirement is that you must have enough material to reach a 'critical mass', if I may pinch that term from physics. When this point is reached it's time to assemble the heap properly, or to give it its first 'turn' if you like.

To work well the pile must be built up in rough layers, as near to a sphere or cube as possible, as the greatest amount of the compost needs be in the centre and well insulated for the heating process to work well. A simple wall or fence to contain it helps but you don't need plastic bins, most of which are too small and too badly ventilated anyway. You do, I repeat, need a good size heap but lids, covers and water catching trays are also quite unnecessary clutter. If the material is dry it pays to water it at the start – not too much, just to the point of pleasantly moist is all that's needed.

When the heap is nearly half built it's a good idea to add some of what's called, hot or starter material, into the centre layers. This means anything which is high in nitrogen, or in simple terms soft, fresh and tender. Perhaps the best is fresh grass mowings, which should be mixed with about an equal amount of the other ingredients in the very centre of the heap. Don't dilute them too much because we need their heat but we don't want them compacting in a solid slimy lump either.

If you have no grass, then animal manure will do as well, almost any except horse manure which tends to be too cold; even the dried pelleted manure in bags from the garden centre will help. If you don't have any hot matter to hand you could try a so-called compost activator which you can also buy at the garden centre, though it's perfectly possible to make the heap work without it, so you might as well save your money. Some people use their own urine, which is excellent, especially when mixed with three or four times the amount of water and sprinkled on the centre of the heap – but only if you're brave enough to use a bucket in the garden! In this respect men do have a natural but still unfair advantage, which means they tend not to need the bucket, and since the method is fairly obvious, it needn't be discussed too deeply here. But gentlemen at least you now know what it's useful for...

There are some ingredients however, that I'd certainly leave out, especially as there has been a lot of bad advice given on building hot heaps. Sometimes in the past it was recommended that you should build the heap up with layers of soil, which were supposed to introduce the necessary bacteria; and layers of lime to correct the acidity. The problem with both these inert minerals is that they dilute the compost and make it less likely to heat up well, it pays therefore to be very circumspect about their use. A little lime may in fact help if sprinkled on the layers, especially if you garden on a neutral to acid soil but it isn't essential, and especially not if your soil naturally contains chalk or limestone – there should be more than enough alkaline matter on the roots of the weeds to keep the heap 'sweet', as the 'compost connoisseurs' say. By which they mean that the best bacteria, those that make the heat, thrive best in alkaline conditions, while acid conditions encourage the microbes, which make bad odours.

Modern compost makers have however entirely rejected the practice of adding soil to the pile as there's no need at all to inoculate the heap with bacteria; there are plenty of good bacteria everywhere in the garden waste and some soil on the weed roots, so don't worry. Sadly of course it was mistaken ideas like these being widely propagated which destroyed many people's attempts at the hot compost method, and made it seem like a magical process only achievable by gardening wizards with long grey beards and a magic wheelbarrow.

**

Anyway you should then continue loading the waste until you've finished your heap. When you have a nice large pile, moist and full of air, never be tempted to press it down as you need all the air it can hold, and it will settle quite soon enough. Then all you need to do is to wait, and not for very long. Within a few days the heap should start to heat, cooking from the centre outwards, which is why you need a good sized pile initially because the waste on the outside provides the centre with its insulation. And if the heap warms in the centre even slightly, the bacteria will start to grow and work faster, and the more there are and the faster they work the more heat they'll produce, which will hopefully lead to a runaway explosion of heat and bacteria! Eventually the heat will rise to a point where even the outside of the heap feels warm to the touch, and it will probably steam in cold weather, though it will never smell.

The real heat, however, the heat that matters and gets the job done, will be in the centre, and if you thrust a strong thin cane or metal rod in to it for a minute or two, you'll find that when removed it will be hot to the touch, while if the heap is working really well it will be almost unbearably hot so that you have to pull your hand away quickly. This is the organic bonfire at work. And the great advantage of attempting to make a hot compost heap by this modern method is that even if you fail, then in the fallback position, you'll simply have an ordinary cold compost heap which is exactly what you would have had anyway, and no worse because of it.

When the heat has at last gone, you may then open the heap and see what you've made. If the heating has done its work well, then you should find soft brown crumbling compost (as fine as any you could buy in bags from the garden centre) at the heart of the heap. If the heap has worked very well indeed then you may even find that some of the vegetable waste in the very centre is reduced to a fine white material much like bonfire ash, and it is in fact not very much different from ash. Both of these may be used straight away on the garden if you wish.

The remainder of the heap from around the outside, and any coarse, un-rotted stuff can then be used as the start of the next heap, and if you're not quite ready to use your compost, then just follow the old traditional practice of turning the heap once more and starting the whole process all over again. This time, however, you put the well-composted matter from the inside onto the outside, as insulation for the un-rotted matter which came from the outside. That way all the waste you've built the heap with gets to enjoy a good heating in the centre.

**

Now it's at this point that a lot of people will hold their hands up in alarm and start talking foolishly about 'all this turning' being a huge amount of work, the supposed large amount of labour being an objection to this method of compost making, an objection that is both tedious and over-conventionalised, so much so, that hearing it always makes me want to yawn. It's such a silly argument.

To begin with you have to remember that to get your garden waste to the compost heap in the first place, you'll have already handled it once into the wheelbarrow, and once out of it. You'll then (whatever method you use) handle it twice more when you return it to the garden, so that a single turning only makes up a fifth of the whole effort at the very most, and without even the need to push the barrow.

But what's even sillier is the fact that we live in a world where people worry all the time about lack of exercise and the negative effects that it has on health, as a consequence of which we happily pay hundreds of pounds a year to use health clubs and the like, to put us on treadmills and make us run like mindlessly inbred laboratory mice.

Yet we think that an hour spent in the fresh air with a fork while listening to the birdsong, watching the wildlife go by, enjoying the gentle challenge of sorting our compost into the usable, and that which needs another turn, with a chance of observing and speculating on the behaviour and ecology of bacteria and all the other small life, while we do so; as hard work. Which is why it's good to write things for gardeners because I know that you at least are wiser than that. Keep in mind that it takes a very large garden indeed to make a ton of compost, an amount which a fit person should be able to turn in fifteen minutes or someone rather more frail or elderly may take an hour over. So what then will you then do for your half hour's recommended exercise, the other three hundred and sixty four days of the year?

So what at last are the advantages of a hot heap over the ordinary cold type, now that you have gone to this tiny amount of extra trouble and care to make one? Well, you'll have your compost faster, and therefore also from much less space. There's little need for the bins and covers that are sold in the garden centres as 'aids' to compost making, so you can save the trouble and cost of them. You'll also be able to use a much greater percentage of your waste because the hot heap will cook even quite tough woody materials thoroughly, and those that it doesn't can simply be put in again for another turn. This means therefore that when once you've mastered it, even tough perennial weeds and their roots, normally excluded from the compost pile by most cold composting pundits, can be composted, while there is next to no chance of diseases or pests surviving the process, so that your compost is far safer to use.

But perhaps the main advantage of all is quite simply the sheer joy and fun of it. When you pull out the cane or metal rod probe from the heap's centre, and find that it's blazing hot, too hot to bear your hand on, you'll then realise the meaning of the term 'organic bonfire' which is often used for the hot method. You should feel a rich sense of achievement and you'll learn much in real practical terms about the lives of the common garden microbes. While if you are a person of any imagination at all, that little bit of practical experience will impress you with a sense of their power and potential, far more deeply than any amount of academic study. But what really matters most of all is the pure pleasure and joy of it, easily the equal of making a conventional bonfire, but without the smoke.

Inspired by this, you may even become a keen enthusiastic heap builder, wanting to expand your skills and try ever greater challenges, such as composting shredded hedge trimmings, while the green recycling bin from the council can find a new use for storing tools or some other purpose. You may I think, still want a bonfire, and why not, but I guarantee you won't pine too much for it.

Showing

Garden shows aren't perhaps the most important part of the nursery's year but they're certainly in some ways the natural peak. Though the show itself only lasts from two to four days, they often take up a good part of a week or more for the nurseryman. The whole business begins some days, or even weeks before the show day, with the admittedly pleasant and tranquil task of wandering slowly among your greenhouses, quietly sorting through the best of your stock in search of the plants which you hope will impress the judges on the show bench.

Maybe this one is a good one? It looks nice from the top, but no, it's too bare at the bottom. Or this one? No, not enough good leaves when all the second-rate ones have been trimmed off. But in the end you only need a few really good ones anyway, and you always end up picking out too many and then have to harden your heart and put some back. Maybe we can show that one next year instead?

The work only begins in real earnest, however, when you arrive at the show ground. Outside the show pavilion everything appears to be hustle and unruly haste in the car park, with people jostling for the best parking places nearest their sites, then manoeuvring giant, top heavy and unstable trollies of plants in and out of the rows of vehicles.

Within the pavilion itself though, there is a complete and striking contrast. Here the work, which is essentially just giant flower arranging, takes the form of intense, earnest and largely quiet endeavour of just the sort that the serious ladies in the flower tent next door generally undertake, with many little groups working away at their displays, each in semi isolation from the other. Only occasionally is the half quiet broken by the odd raucous laugh, loud curse or little giggle, but even that rarely breaks the close concentration of the workers.

Apart from the human voices, the only other sounds common to the day are those of hammers and saws banging and grating away, for lack of space in vehicles and the difficulty of accessing electrical power on site means that showing must be one of the very last major activities where power tools play little part, and one of the few you will still see hand crafting in earnest.

The nursery people however usually try their best to give the entirely false impression that they are altogether too well organised for rushing, and despite the urgency imposed by the show schedule, some part of each day can still found for the exchange of gossip and humour. Not to mention the all-important encouragement and advice if it's needed, for thankfully this is a friendly trade where even earnest competitors support each other, often exchanging plants and tools all the while they're competing.

Stands built by the nurseries come in three basic flavours: the 'plain vanilla' style is to set up a display of the blooms cut from your plants and placed in vases, effectively as flower arrangements. This naturally tends to be the choice of those nurseries that grow bulbs, or cutting flowers such as daffodils and chrysanthemums. The second more 'Neapolitan' style of stand consists of growing plants displayed in pots, usually on benching tiered in steps from front to back. There is of course a little more to it than that, since the benching must be covered with cloth or gravel, and it requires a drapery background, while everything including both plants and pots must be as immaculate as possible. The cheat, as you might guess, is to conceal the pots which the plants are grown in at the nursery inside larger, cleaner and more decorative pots for the duration of the show.

The full 'ice cream sundae' style however, is to compose a complete miniature landscape on the stand, where the pots are completely concealed by moss, bark, leaves and other materials to give the impression that they're growing, just as they would in the garden or wild nature. This is the sort of stand we always build, much to the mild annoyance of my father, whom I catch every so often looking wistfully at the other stands, while he makes a comment about how much easier it would all be if we only had to drop a few plants into pots. "Yes," I reply, "but we aim to impress the public as well as the judges and show them what they could do in their gardens. We can also display more plants this way, and maintaining, storing and transporting lots of heavy pots is just as difficult and expensive."

But in fact, the fresh moss is green, moist and pleasant to handle, and reminds me of the outdoors; the dry leaves remind me of last autumn when I collected them and stored them carefully in the shed for the winter, and my precious cork bark imported from Portugal which we use to simulate logs is always a pleasure to handle. In the end, a replica of a woodland floor slowly appears on top of a pile of empty plant pots and milk crates which form the ground beneath, and it always seems to turn out better than I'd hoped, just as if someone else had done it. The fact is I like doing it this way.

The pace quickens and everything becomes ever more earnest on the last day before the show, as time begins to run out. Soon the stewards will be calling on everyone to vacate the pavilion so that the all-important judging may take place. There are always a few competitors who have their stands completed well ahead of time. They're already long gone and left for home, but most of us are working away into the dark, still managing to find a few last minute things that desperately need doing, and there are always a few who seem to relish the challenge of turning up as late as they can and rushing like mad to finish. One man, who shows violets, likes to build his stand entirely out of real bricks, with walls and herringbone paving. He's generally one of the last to arrive, and spends most of the night laying hundreds of bricks, even before he puts his plants out.

**

But finally time is up and everyone drifts slowly out, before the stewards push us out, empting the pavilion and leaving the vast plant-filled space that was just a few minutes before so busy, and now completely silent and vacant: the mysterious arts and rituals of judging may now take place undisturbed. As the last few of us leave – apart from the odd someone who always has to rush back to grab their van keys or a straying and willful broom – the pavilion, in contrast to the earlier bustle, is eerily rather still and filled with a cool green gloom as though even the plants are waiting for some great event.
Whenever I stop to think about it, this sort of competition seems to be a totally strange if not unique activity, it being perhaps the only sport I know (if sport it is) where the points are awarded after the competitors have left the arena and gone home.
The show nurseries form a sort of gypsy community always on the move, meeting, parting and meeting again in yearly cycles; all the old, well- established faces at all the old, well-established and seasonal camp sites. There are, it seems, two sorts of nursery people who attend shows – those who see the show mainly as a way to promote their nurseries and put them before a wider public, with sales and prize money hopefully covering their expenses, and those for whom showing is their main activity, who aim to sell most or all of their plants at these shows. These people are the true floating community, always on the move, often going directly from

one show to the next, and these are the ones most likely to be camping out on the show grounds. As a result, when the other nursery people return in the early morning for the first of the show days, the approach resembles a tented camp, and smells richly with the appetising aroma of frying bacon, steaming tea and all the strong smells of morning in the open air.

**

On show days the nursery people are allowed into the show well ahead of time for what is called the 'restocking hour', when plants that are to be offered to the public for sale may be brought in and placed behind the stands. This is the truly magical time when the work of assembly is complete but the work of advising, selling and promoting to the public is not yet begun. At this time, the pavilion is always cool and humid, a deep forest morning cool filled with the scents of earth and plants. And for just a short while, the show belongs to the tradespeople exclusively.

The hour passes altogether too quickly, with people hurrying in all directions carrying watering cans, for the show is not only the last tenuous bastion of hand tools but also perhaps the last place where the watering of plants is still done entirely by hand. People busily swing heavy metal cans with giant brass roses, while hand sprays are vigorously pumped to fill the already humid air with extra mist. Busy as everyone is though, there's still time for people to collect in groups and exchange gossip with old acquaintances: "No they won't be here. He broke his leg and they decided to retire a year early". "Wrigglington Show was dire, hardly anyone about, I shan't be going there again." "Got anything new this year?" "I brought you a bit of this, you remember you asked me about it last March." Such a special time.

Meanwhile stands are admired, ideas are exchanged, and (of course!) judgment pronounced on the judges; sometimes, but only occasionally, you even feel that this ritual of counter-judgment has more than just a faint trace of justification. This year I might talk for a while to Mr Simms, a jolly and eager character who will try to persuade me of the benefits of his latest money-making scheme. Or perhaps to Mrs Andrew, a generously-built, gentle, genial woman who, as usual, is accompanied by Mrs Bolt, a small, cheerful and bright lady with a button nose and large round glasses. I remember when I was new and eager for show success, I naturally poured heart and soul into my first stand, and was also (quite naturally for the inexperienced) disappointed with my medal. "Don't worry," said these two ladies, with eyes twinkling, "it will come, you see." And of course they were right, it did.

**

Soon the doors open and we're ready for business. The first hour or two are always slow as they are for looking only – nobody buys anything until they've had a good look round. So the nursery owners have to wait a while to find out if all their efforts are going to be rewarded. But soon comes the first little dribble of sales, then a rush, and a wild melée soon ensues as you try to answer a question, hand out a catalogue, wrap a plant and give change
to four different people all at once; all the while trying to behave like the skilled diplomat that you wish you were, often in the face of almost impossible enquiries.

But at least you can amuse yourself by keeping a running count of how often you have to answer the same questions, especially the almost ubiquitous. "Why did my 'x...' die?" To which the truly honest answers of: " I don't know as I can't see your garden from here." or "I don't know, they're really very tough and I've never managed to kill one myself," seem not to answer the problem, at least not very diplomatically. And so I must resort to a long and detailed enquiry into the history of the plant, followed by (hopefully!) an inspired guess, all of which could have been helped quite easily if anyone ever thought to bring a sample with them, which of course they never do, but at least the customer departs with a happy smile, and hopefully they'll have the optimism and confidence to try again. One final thought is that I sometimes think that the ones who are told: "I always fail with that. I've never found a way to keep it alive," are the ones who go away looking the happiest.

Sometimes the visitors provide you with great amusement or horror, and sometimes both, often without even intending it. As with the two ladies who walked past the stall one day and said, "Mm, I like ferns a lot. Do you know I think they would look really good in your garden." "Yes, so do I," replied the second. "You mean under the trees at the bottom?" "That's right." "Yes, that would be a really good job for this weekend, we could plant the whole area up. I'll get George to get the car out, and we'll go down to the woods and dig some up."

But for the most part the public at such times only ever impresses you with the great kindness and thoughtfulness of people; those who will bring you the gift of a cutting or seedling, probably from a plant that you only mentioned in a brief snatch of conversation, perhaps as much as a whole year ago, at the last show. Or the person who wishes to share with you the knowledge of how to grow some difficult species, and their modest pride in the achievement. Consequently, when you get a rare spare moment, you have an excuse to visit the bonsai show where one of your plants takes pride of place in someone else's exhibit, nestled with the greatest of care beneath a perfectly formed miniature tree.

**

For a few days the show is both your life, your home and all that you can think about. Then quite suddenly, on the final day, with hardly any warning, the whole thing is cleared away in just a couple of rushed hours. And the floating world that is the show community smiles, laughs and calls out its temporary farewells, bangs its van doors and disappears as though it had never been there, only to reassemble again, in a different form and mixture in some other place, perhaps no more than a day or two later.
Yet all is not entirely well with the shows. Year after year sales are down; the garden centre and the mail order business, aided by the Internet, provide the public with ever more and more easier ways to spend their garden budget without travelling all the way to a show. Gardens get smaller and filled with paving slabs, and it becomes increasingly expensive and, in an environmentally aware age, less acceptable for both the public and the exhibitors to travel long distances just for a flower show. It may be that we live in the last few years of the traditional garden show, or at least that the smaller shows will soon begin to close, then showing will become a much more exclusive and rare thing. Maybe since it is for the public only one of the smaller parts of their gardening life, and the nursery people will be busy mailing their plants out in boxes, possibly the passing of the garden show will be all but unnoticed. I wonder.

Snowdrops And Churchyards

Recently I took a friend to one of the newly fashionable events called snowdrop days where certain public gardens, normally only open in the high summer, make an early attempt (despite often unreliable seasons and weather) to grab a little winter income by opening a few days each spring during the snowdrop season. Hopefully cashing in on the current high fashion status of the small and familiar but quite enchanting white flowers.

My friend and I were unfortunately a little disappointed by what we found – not in the gardens which were pleasant and the snowdrops were the perfect white bells they should be, while the weather was the best sort of bright crisply-aired winter's day you can get. No, what really disappointed us was that the bulb displays seemed to be thin and poor in quantity, if not quality. They'd obviously been planted quite deliberately just a few years before, covering only a few selected places in the gardens, and had then been allowed only a year or so to mature, with little extra attention since.

We didn't complain, of course, because the entrance money was for a good cause, and we're both wise enough or at least old enough to know that everything is relative. Had we been newly arrived from some bleak country where snowdrops don't grow, I'm certain we would have found even one delicate white bell nodding in the winter breeze quite wonderful. Unfortunately however, my friend and I have been slightly spoiled in snowdrop terms, expecting far more than is reasonable. So having refreshed ourselves with the obligatory cake and tea which generally appears at these events, we decided to spoil ourselves as we wended our way homewards, by visiting a churchyard we know in a neighbouring parish, which is largely responsible for our spoiling.

**

We stopped the car on a narrow patch of grass verge sandwiched between some trees and a drystone retaining wall, just big enough to hold a car plus a small post box and an old red telephone kiosk, the latter now hardly used in this age of mobile phones and the internet. The churchyard itself is raised to shoulder height above the level of the road and held in place by the aforementioned drystone retaining wall in the shade of tall trees. In consequence the wall has long since become covered with moss and turned into a pile of green velvet cushions. You don't therefore, get a full view of the church's plot until after you've climbed a few steps and passed through a small iron gate.

When once you're up there, however, you might well think that you've made some great athletic accomplishment rather than just climbed a few steps, because the ground on either side of the path has been carpeted with a marvellously rich and colourful display, equally as good as the flower-filled podiums used to celebrate the achievements of great public heroes and sporting stars.

The ground between the gravestones in this otherwise humble little country churchyard is filled with an almost perfectly random mixture of brilliant white snowdrops and bright yellow winter aconites. You can wander where you wish on this small plot, and with every corner turned you find a yet thicker covering of flowers than before. This wonderfully rich spectacle is the reason why my friend and I regard ourselves as perhaps a little bit spoilt; it's hard not to compare what we can see here for no cost with the much less splendid efforts of the gardens we'd just visited.

To be fair to the gardeners though, I should point out that it would take many years to achieve the sort of display that this churchyard has no doubt been developing naturally over many decades, if not centuries. Even if you're given a large number of bulbs to plant in the beginning and use the technique of dividing each clump a little every three or four years, (a method often used by patient snowdrop growers to improve their display) you'd still take some decades to match this.

And the wonderful thing is that despite the undoubted length of the timescale, neither the snowdrops nor the aconites have yet come to dominate the area alone, neither of them out competing its partner, nor stealing all the ground. Instead they seem to have found a moderately harmonious balance so that the ground beneath your feet is an almost perfect random mixture of yellow and white. It's impossible to say whether this will always be the case, but it certainly is so far, and given that the plants seem to have quite different styles of foliage and growth, it's possible to imagine that they can both find some sort of separate niche even within the small plot and narrow spring growing season. So assuming that the churchyard remains undisturbed, and the trees surrounding it un-felled, then it's possible that travellers may still enjoy a similar spectacle in a century from now, or even longer.

In the end, my friend and I agreed, that for the sake of fairness we should say that we'd enjoyed two good displays that day, one the work of gardeners and the other the work of some unknown person, plus rich deep time and the limitless patience of nature.

**

The truth is, however, that such semi-natural displays are not all that uncommon in Britain – you probably know of at least one or two near your own home. The real surprise however is that, though the carpets of snowdrops and aconites in our woods may appear to be wild, it's generally thought that neither plant is truly native. When the Celts and the Saxons stalked the forests in search of the wild game to supplement their hard arable diet in the hungry dormant season, the winter woods they encountered would hardly have shown a single blossom to relieve the browns and greys. Possibly the only brightness then to be found would have come from the evergreens, the holly and the ivy with their berries and shining leaves. It's no wonder therefore that those two shrubs form such a large part of the older Christmas traditions, but not those strange newcomers the snowdrop or the aconite who are too recently arrived. In fact virtually all the displays of snowdrop and aconite you see will have had a helping hand from humans at some stage in just the last thousand years or so.

This isn't really so surprising since the snowdrop has made life difficult for itself by flowering very early in the year, well before many pollinators can possibly be on the wing this far north. But also its method for distributing its seeds once they're set is a questionable one, since it tries to recruit ants by coating its seeds with a rich fatty covering which the ants find extremely tasty. That, however, can never have been a reliable strategy in Britain where ants are not at their most numerous or active early in the summer when the snowdrops' stem finally goes down; however successful it may be in southern Europe where it's thought the snowdrop originated. Certainly relying on ants is not likely to have been a very good idea in Britain anyway because our woodlands have been so fragmented since at least the early Middle Ages, that finding two woods connected by the same ant colony would be almost like winning the lottery.

The snowdrop does its best, however, to make the most of its lot, the flowers like those of most winter flowers, being extremely long lasting, giving it plenty of time to attract the sparse pollinators of late winter. Nor is it any accident that the snowdrop forms its flowers in the shape of hanging bells because this helps to protect the vital centres against the worst of the winter weather; and to guarantee the continued shelter whatever the blow, they're made to swing slightly with the wind.

Hanging flowers seem to be a common strategy for winter blooming plants – hellebores for example, to the slight annoyance of many gardeners, persistently hang their heads through most of the winter. Their strategy, however, is a little more subtle than the snowdrop's because as the season moves towards spring and the time for damage to occur passes, they slowly raise their heads to meet the sun. Flowers with their face turned down would naturally be difficult for insects to find but with that simple action, the hellebore contrives to get the best of both endurance and display, maximising its chances of catching the rare winter pollinators, yet risking more exposure as the insects themselves become bolder and the weather tempers towards the spring.

The snowdrop, however, remains determinedly facing down but increases its chances of attracting attention by colouring the back of its flower as brightly as the front, and having only a light thin brown cover to the flower which slides back well out of the way when the bloom opens. By far the best of all the snowdrop's stratagems, though, has been to recruit human beings to help its spread; it's almost certainly human help alone which helped them become established in just about every parish and every county.

**

And why should it seem less romantic anyway that the snowdrop is not a native flower? If you're prepared to use your imagination then every flower has a history to tell of its relationships with our predecessors. Nobody is quite sure when snowdrops began their relationship with the British people – according to popular legend they were first spread by medieval nuns and monks who regarded them as a symbol of holy chastity, if not virginity.

But like most folklore, this story seems to me to be just a little too neat. Yes, I know that in medieval times the church held a virtual monopoly on decorative horticulture, and almost anything pleasant that added value to life. And no doubt the flowers that managed to escape the cloister into the secular world often did so by night, or were carefully secreted by trembling hands beneath a pile of rubbish. Yet nature was always available and some small scraps of green must surely have been passed round in a spirit of generosity even wider and older than that of the church.

The snowdrop especially must have been highly valued by anyone in those not so distant ages before electric light or synthetic dyes, when the only bright colours most people ever encountered came from birds, berries, insects and flowers, most of which disappeared for months on end in the darkest and most dismal period of the year when the fields and woods showed only the greys and browns of death and dormancy. Until at long last, when people had almost despaired of any brightness, the snowdrop flowered. How prized then would be a bright splash of living white light, no matter how humble you were, you surely couldn't leave it only in the churchyard?

The snowdrops in the churchyard of our neighbouring parish, however, may well have come originally from a monastery, since the parish lies within the estates of an ancient abbey, and it's quite likely that the bulbs were handed down from the original medieval stock. This is not so improbably romantic an idea as it may sound, since until the motor car gave country people freedom of movement, and with that access to the marvels of the garden centre, they would have seen no benefit in fetching things further than you had to, and most of the plants that circulated were probably handed down within the parish.

The familiar bright yellow winter aconite (which is no relation to the true aconite) is an even more recent introduction than the snowdrop, cohabiting with us for perhaps less than a couple of centuries. It's most probable therefore that both the flowers were introduced into the churchyard, possibly at the same time, by someone in the nineteenth or early twentieth centuries, when the idea of 'naturalising', as gardeners call it, was first in vogue; some fifty years or so being the minimum time I would estimate needed to make this sort of display.

**

Which means that, if my not very speculative guesses are correct, the floral display we enjoyed that day is not just a gift of nature and a happy accident but is the result of a long and complex human heritage which started at least as early as the Middle Ages. Some

travelling pedlar or clergy must have transported the bulbs from another parish, or even country perhaps far to the south where the winters were less harsh. He would have carried them carefully as a precious treasured cargo intended to impress the pious with the beneficence of god and the church's wisdom, a special clerical treasure, too valuable to grace anywhere but the abbey cloister.
Or just maybe they came as a gift, a rare luxury for some wealthy member of the medieval upper classes, sent by a friend or admirer, maybe stolen or perhaps bought at some market for no small amount of hard-earned money. They were then planted out and treasured for a while, then perhaps in time lost to cultivation, to wars, plagues and the Reformation which destroyed at least the old abbey in the next village utterly so that not a stone now remains.
But some of the bulbs survived, passed from cottage garden to cottage garden, sometimes for a while abandoned and having to shift for themselves in a wild hedgerow before being lifted again and replanted. Until at last some public-spirited person, in the post-romantic era when naturalising had become popular, knew where they could find a stock of bulbs to dig up and divide, and thought that naturalised snowdrops would beautify the churchyard. Transplanting them there, along with some of the then newly-imported aconites, to grow, spread, increase and be admired for who knows how long into the future. And if all of this tale should be a little fanciful in detail, then it's least true in general outline. And anyway I know of few better stories to tell you.

Sowing Spores

It always seems natural to assume that the very heart of the season in every plant nursery is the time of propagation, when the first investment is made to produce the stock for future years. It's a little harder to say why it should seem so natural to regard this as the heart, as the potting up of small plants into larger pots adds more value more quickly, and the selling of plants is the ultimate aim. But propagation is for some reason almost invariably a solitary pursuit usually performed by just one or two people alone with the plants, and it perhaps seems natural that solitude should always be found at the very heart of things.

Propagation at a fern nursery is slightly different from that at most nurseries because of the slightly different biology of ferns. If I asked you what you can remember about ferns from your schooldays, then the first thing that may possibly come to mind is the memory that these are early plants whose history goes back very nearly to the beginnings of life on land. And if you're anything like me you'll have a vaguely remembered impression of a dog-eared school textbook and its old lithographic illustration of a carboniferous rain forest, complete with a primitive amphibian, a giant dragonfly and towering tree ferns. While if your memory serves you very well, then you'll probably also recall that ferns pre-date the origins of seeds and flowers, reproducing themselves via spores, as do the mosses, liverworts and most of the plants which have come down to us from deep time.

**

So that if you pick a spring day and look on the underside of a typical fern frond, especially if it's quite a large mature frond, you'll see some things that look very much like warts, structures botanists call sori. These structures have an outer cover like a blister called the indusia, which it should be pointed out, are not simply round blobs, they're varied enough in shape for botanists to use them as characters to divide one genera of ferns from another. If you look closely you'll find that they possess a quite elaborate architecture, some being shaped like shields, others like bladders, kidneys, sausages or hockey sticks; and just for good measure if the fern you've picked is a Polypodium then you'll find it has no indusia at all,

and the structures beneath are quite naked to your eye.
Later in the summer the indusia will split open and curl up because they're merely the covers for the truly vital organs beneath, called sporangia which now show through, and it's these that produce the spores of the fern. Take a hand lens, if you will, and look closely at these parts and you'll find that they're as complex and beautiful as the flowers of a tropical orchid but only one tenth of the size.
The sporangia, which look like tiny bobbles on stalks, are designed to act like little pepper pots; when finally mature they will open at the ends to release the spores. If you've a strong lens or your eye is very good, you may see some large thick cells on the tips of the bobbles called annulus cells, and this is where the split takes place. The fern however does not just rely on allowing the spores to fall out, instead the sporangia are set on a stalk and as the temperature and humidity change in the course of a day, the stalk gradually bends, building up tension; it then snaps back, giving a real pepper pot-like action to the sporangia. If you bring a frond into the house and put it near a warm light bulb, you can sometimes see the sporangia in action with just a lens and a little patience, though a low power microscope gives a much better view, and if you're a person who is sensitive to such things, you'll be as impressed as I always am by how violently active apparently passive plants can be when nature demands it of them.
And it's this that occupies what are perhaps the best of my summer's days pottering quietly round my garden, scissors in hand, turning over the fronds of ferns to see if they're ready to shed their spores yet. Then if they are I'll snip off a piece and put it in an envelope. The envelopes will then go to the potting shed where they'll be placed in a box to dry out and shed their spores, which usually takes about a week.

**

The spores are, of course, no more than single plant cells in a coating, which means that they're extremely vulnerable, and when sown it takes them quite a while to grow during which time they can easily be overwhelmed by any growths of moss, alga or fungi. In the wild, perhaps less than one in a million succeed in growing but the gardener hopes for a lot better than that, since you cannot sow a whole woodland floor to get the plants you need. It's therefore necessary to grow the spores in a sterile environment so that they'll have no competition. Which means growing them under carefully cleaned covers and sterilising the compost with boiling water. This is perhaps not a great deal of fun as it involves standing in the potting shed by a large steaming boiler in some of the hottest months of the year but there's always the 'sweat' smell of cooked soil as a reward for your efforts, if nothing else.

When the compost is cooled the fresh spores are sown onto the surface and left to germinate beneath dustproof covers. After a week or two the surface of the compost starts to turn green, and within a few months the first little plants can be seen. But these aren't ferns or anything that resembles them, for the fern is a plant with two stages in its life cycle (like a caterpillar and a butterfly) and what grows from the spore is not a fern but a little simple leaf-like plant called a prothallus.

The prothallus doesn't look in the least like a fern, being no more than a single, nearly flat leaf, easily mistaken for a small liverwort, stuck to the floor by little white root hairs and never much more than a centimetre across. But the prothallus is none the less, the mature, sexually active part in the fern's life cycle. When the prothallus is fully grown it produces male and female sex organs on its underside, Antheridium and Archegonium.

The antheridium, which are the male parts, soon release free-swimming sperm – in nature into the dew and rain of the forest floor but in the nursery they must make use of the moist compost which we keep damp for them. Although these have the same function as animal sperm they do look somewhat different, with stiff coiled tails and with a much more stately way of swimming. Despite which they do eventually manage to fertilise the egg cells of another prothallus, then, usually in a year or so from the spore landing, a new fern will begin to grow. When this happens the prothallus has completed its whole purpose in life, and will wither and die completely, leaving behind – usually within two to three years of the spore landing – a small maturing fern plant known in botanical terms, for obvious reasons, as the sporophyte generation (because it's the stage which sheds the spores).

This of course must then enjoy careful hardening off as it is moved on from the sheltered environment that the spores were sown in, but from that point onwards the fern is grown on in the nursery in much the same way as any young plant which gardeners will know, it only requires more patience in the early stages.

What Lurks In The Shed

You could perhaps manage a garden, or a nursery even, without a potting shed. Some nurseries use movable trailers behind tractors as potting benches or give up a small space in the corner of a greenhouse: everything under one roof, very efficient. We, however, are depressingly old fashioned and enjoy the several minor practical advantages and comforts, (a better climate for humans) of having a potting shed at the very heart of the business.

But in addition to all the practical advantages, I've also discovered that it brings with it one enormous social bonus which I could never have foreseen. For some reason people truly love the potting shed and seem to think it some sort of special privilege when they enter it, as though it were a deep inner sanctum of some pilgrimage site dedicated to the demi-gods of gardening.

Yet in reality (as I suspect most sheds are), it is simply a museum of things that eventually proved useless and experiments that failed. Just to the right of the door, for example, is the heap of tools that I never use, which rests on top of the heap of tools that my father never quite got round to wearing out, and beneath that comes an even larger pile, only partly used by great-grandparents, and whose inscriptions on faded labels (written of course in pounds shillings and pence and other ancient glyphs) betray their immemorial age.

Also just inside the door is a store of bee-keeping equipment, a powered hacksaw, some empty jars which may be useful one day, a sack barrow used for moving tree ferns, another sack barrow never used for anything much, and a garden roller – a tool that no one has ever found a use for.

Next comes a set of pigeonholes filled with a great many nearly redundant labels, all of which were bought long ago from horticultural printing companies in the days before we had a computer and the power to print our own labels in our own words. I often think about throwing them out, but they do occasionally get used when we're in a hurry, so I think they'll eventually be used up given enough time but it does seem to take a very long time indeed.

Next to that is the bottles shelf – well, the only official one anyway – where you could find most of the noxious chemicals known to man, all used at some time but never quite used up. There are also some genuinely useful bottles of bleach for cleaning and sterilising, and most of all a store of spirit vinegar which we use to correct the lime

in our tap water and thereby prevent limescale on plant leaves. You can of course buy chemicals from the wholesalers to do this but we find that the vinegar is not only safer to handle but also a lot cheaper per litre of treated water to use.
Then comes the potting area proper: first the gravel tray filled with grit which is used to top dress pots of plants, especially when moss is cleaned off the surface of the compost on plants that have been left a little too long. Next is the true potting bench, made of an old butcher's table raised up on blocks. It has a huge top, haunted by woodworm and thick enough to make six ordinary tabletops.
Above this is a shelf for essential tools such as scissors, old knives recycled from the kitchen, hammers, two trowels, (one cheap and bendy that I bought in a shop, and a good one specially made by a blacksmith), a riddle, and dibbers et cetera and an electric fan for use in hot summers, ('Hardly ever used, going cheap to good home...').
A wheelbarrow for waste sits parked permanently below the bench among the empty bags and seed trays, and then comes the bin for potting compost, made out of breezeblocks, with a set of shelves above it which form a sort of orphanage for lost and oddly sized pots. And finally on the left hand side there comes the pots bin proper, which holds large stacks of shiny new pots.
The back wall meanwhile holds the writing bench with the label racks, the telephone and a calendar above it. There's usually just enough clear space on it to do a little writing, though you wouldn't want to start anything ambitious such as a novel, because the bench also has to find room for spare price labels arranged in plant pots, reading glasses, (both my father's and mine, though no one is sure whose is whose), note pad, record book, cash tin, an out tray for finished mail orders, tape measure, scissors, receipts book, two plant pots full of pens, (one for fine writing and one for waterproof felt tips), a clock and an ancient radio which despite the digital age still just manages to pick up Classic FM.
There's also a road atlas which may seem a surprising item but it is in fact essential for checking addresses when we're doing mail orders since the people who order plants generally seem to have three things in common, one of which is that they always live in towns and villages with strange names, (and there are a lot of these in Britain), they always have an odd handwriting style, and English is almost certainly never their first language.
Next to the writing bench are the shelves that contain other mail

order things such as cardboard boxes, bags, old newspaper for padding, plus sticky tape and a tape dispenser, while space is also found here for things needed at the shows such as table covers, portable signs, display label holders and boxes of leaflets. Finally come the shelves for all the irrigation equipment – hoses, sprinklers, spare pipe and all types of water fittings. I don't know why, or whether you find this, but it always seems to me that whether you're a full or part-time gardener, the watering part always seems to involve lots of bits and pieces, most of which never get used or are eventually thrown away.

Lastly in the centre of the floor there's a home-made gas boiler used to produce hot water for cleaning and sterilising, plus a multi-purpose stand made from old pallets, a couple of watering cans and two old garden chairs, with several cushions, (no two alike). Which just about completes the inventory, apart from the homes of innumerable spiders, several frogs and toads, the odd stray bird, a winter roost of wrens, and one very lively shrew who may perhaps have raised a family but we never found the nest. Which just leaves the great eternal mystery, which is: Why do people think our potting shed is so interesting? (Especially Mr Summerfield from Westshores Nurseries who insisted on taking photographs and then went away smiling and chuckling to himself?) I suspect only fellow gardeners might know the answer to that one...

Cuttings

Many years ago a neighbouring farmer came to me and asked me if I could help him. He wished to plant a new hedge across a large field, and having visited a local wholesale nursery, found the cost of hawthorn plants, even there, to be far too much for the length he wanted, and did I know anywhere cheaper? He seemed surprised when, having ascertained that he had a year or two to spare, I said, "Why not raise your own plants?" then explaining the fairly simple method that the nursery he had visited probably used itself. It's always seemed strange to me that people should think that propagating woody plants is somehow difficult, and that doing it yourself is somehow not quite 'normal'.

**

For a while now there's been a gap developing in the trees which screen my garden from the nursery, and I've decided that the best way to fill it would be with a couple of shrubs. However I already have most of the 'can't do without' shrubs I need, and since the new ones will not have a major decorative role to play in the garden, I'll save money by propagating some new plants from those I already have.

It's now autumn, the best time for taking some hardwood cuttings, which is the method I will use for growing the new plants. I don't know why more people don't use this easiest of all methods of propagation. It's quick and cheap, as well as giving you relatively large robust plants from the outset, and it needs no special equipment, no greenhouse, propagator, pots, compost or heating cables – not even a plastic bag. All I'll do in this case, is to take some prunings from two or three of my favourite shrubs, dig a small trench in the ground, slip the prunings in and leave them to get on with it. And that's more or less all there is to it. How easy can it get? And yet it seems that I hardly ever talk to a garden owner who has even tried the method.

It is, of course, the case that most gardeners – especially those with only tiny plots – don't perhaps really need all that many trees and shrubs in any one lifetime. Doubly so if hardy herbaceous perennials are your thing. But I suspect there's more to it than that. For one thing there are so many books on gardening, all of which vie with each other for the gardener's attention, and all of which are naturally trying their very best to appear the most authoritative, always giving the most detailed instructions, and always explaining the most refined methods for doing everything.

Yet perhaps in doing so they sometimes miss a point when they fail to make it clear that most of the many refinements they detail with such care, are in fact just that – extra refinements and nothing more. For however good they may be, most such practices are certainly not essentials. For example, most of the books will tell you that hardwood cuttings are, 'cuttings made of mature wood from the previous season's growth'. Which sounds fine, grand even, and to tell the truth more than a little intimidating. But all that such a phrase really means is that they're cuttings taken mainly in the autumn; and what else except, 'mature wood of the previous season's growth' are you going to find on any bush or tree in the autumn?

The second thing that most books will tell you is that you should put your hardwood cuttings into your seedbed after first preparing a trench at least a spade spit deep, and then putting coarse sand for drainage in the bottom. Well, apart from pointing out that in modern small gardens many people don't have the luxury of purpose-made seedbeds these days, I also must say that this really is truly a refinement too far in many cases. Though coarse sand may increase the number of successful "takes" in some hard-to-root shrubs and trees, and is perhaps helpful on wet and poor draining soils, it's still very much an extra because nine out of ten cuttings will root perfectly well without it, and not all of them will take even if you do give them such care. As always in nature, you're dealing with percentages not absolutes.

**

In fact, what I shall do is exactly what generations of country people before me have done. Whenever, for example, they needed a new hedge or some new fruit bushes, they simply thrust some quite crude cuttings into the ground exactly where they wanted the new plants to grow, not even thinking about seed beds. I shall also follow another timeworn path, one long followed by simple-minded rustics like me: in order to ensure that I get a cutting to take in every place that I need one, I shall put into the trench far more cuttings than are needed. If you use prunings as cuttings anyway, they'll have cost nothing, and this saves the need to bonfire them. Then eventually, next year maybe, if I'm not too lazy, I'll take the spares out, or being

very lazy, I'll just let them grow into a tangle!
The books, and the modern television pundits, will also make it seem far more difficult by telling you exactly the correct length of a cutting you need, and precisely where to make the cuts. That degree of care can help increase your success rate sometimes it's true, but not often; and it's also true that some shrubs will do better if broken at a joint rather than being cut. And the answer? Use the shotgun approach and do both. If you want proof that this method works, then you need only need go out into the country and look around you, because nearly all the ancient hedges you see in Britain – and once there used to be many thousands of miles of them – were all planted by people who simply stuck into the ground as many of the choppings from an old hedge as they could get their hands on, however they were cut. They stuffed them in together in large numbers, all tangled and jumbled, to make as near an 'instant fence' as they could get from the start, helping therefore to keep the livestock out even before growth began, just by the simple volume of twigs. And it worked. Not only did it keep the animals in their place but enough of the prunings would root eventually to make a solid hedge. Which is what I adviced my farmer friend to do.
Of course, in those days they were using easily rooted material, usually Hawthorn, which was often called Quick Thorn, an old name meaning 'live thorn,' because of the ease with which it could be rooted. Some woody plants are more ready to root than others. Many trees and shrubs already have root initials, or so-called 'adventitious' roots sprouting from around their nodes or leaf joints. Willows, Ivy, Euonymus, Blackcurrants, Cornus and many others all show this character and are therefore among the easiest of shrubs to root. Often the little baby roots are clearly visible, so there's no need to check the books to see if your shrub is easy to root; just look at the plant.
If you haven't seen them before, look for little roots on the wrinkly tissue round the nodes on the stems where the leaves or side branches come out. To see them best, look preferably at a low branch in heavy shade where the rootlets will often be quite large, since in that position they're already getting ready to go. (Oh, and guess which sort of branch it's best to take your cuttings from? Here's a clue; it's not a branch from the top of the bush...)
This should also give you the tip as to where you should make the final cut when you chop them to length. (That is, of course, only if you wish to add another refinement to your method.) If you do take

such cuttings, then there's usually little benefit to be gained from leaving any clear stem below the node, as the roots will almost certainly emerge from the node anyway, and in the long run the spare stem will just rot away, perhaps causing problems for the plant eventually. But that is only a perhaps as it's most probable that the plant will thrive even if you leave the stem. For obvious reasons it also pays to leave only a couple of buds and a few inches of stem above the ground as the new roots will do better if they don't have too much top growth to support at the start, but again don't worry too much – I've used branches with four feet or more of clear stem sticking out of the ground and it still worked.

When I think about it, I owe quite a lot of the plants in the garden to this method, and although I've never been an especially enthusiastic woody plants person – preferring herbs and ferns in my later life especially – still the trees and shrubs raised in this way do make a major contribution to my garden. At the very least my two big silver willows, which form a huge part of my woodland, came from a kind friend's gift of cuttings, and now after twenty years they are huge fifty foot trees which many visitors think must be a century old at least. Most of my shrub roses, too, have been moved from garden to garden as hardwood cuttings, including the lovely 'Alba Celestial' with its soft silver leaves and highly scented pink flowers. Plus my currants, several Euonymus, gooseberries and a Philadelphus – quite a list if I think about it, and none of them took more than an easy half an hour's work.

I always find it amusing to think of the large number of legends, mostly dating from the Middle Ages, which tell the story of how various saints and holy men contrived to prove their holiness by pushing their walking sticks in the ground which then miraculously sprouted into trees. West country legend tells us that Joseph of Arimathea was one of them, and according to one of the commonest stories, he gave the Midland Hawthorn, Crataegus laevigata, to the British in this way.

The method must be really easy, if even Old Joe and I can both do it without really trying. Give it a go next time you need a new shrub or tree!

The Moth Lady

You entered the nursery and garden via a fairly ordinary looking gate leading off a quite normal road, in a pleasant but not especially noteworthy small country town. Nothing about the entrance, close beside an end-of- terrace house, would lead you to believe that anything special lay behind. The drive, in turn, led to a small back yard paved with bricks and even here you wouldn't easily expect that there was anything unusual to be found there. Except that is, if you were a plant enthusiast, when you would perhaps notice that the plants surrounding the little yard were all rather unusual. Moreover, if your knowledge was good, then you'd notice that they were part of a small but very choice collection which included some very rare and special types not often seen, even if you were a regular visitor to quite grand gardens.

And this would perhaps give you a little hint of what was to come: if you were still curious you could then ascend a small flight of steps out of the back of the yard, passing under an iron arch thickly grown with clematis and honeysuckle, both scented to the point of being overwhelming. And just as you thought that the barrage of scent was almost too much to bear, then you'd find – lurking just beyond the arch – a whole new paradise, this time of colour, equally powerful and flooding your eyes with a wide variety and subtlety of shades, from pastel to primary.

**

Beyond the arch was truly an almost secret garden, where broad flower-filled borders left hardly any space for the neatly edged gravel paths that ran between them. The garden was effectively what is called in fashionable language, a 'garden of rooms', being split into many small sections each screened from the others and each having a different character but not pretentiously laid out to any exact plan. It was simply that the space had been so filled with so many different plants that the drifts and clumps of perennials and shrubs formed almost natural divisions, turning you into an explorer and making the quite moderately-sized garden seem truly huge. Not only that but so skillful was the planting that it mattered little what time of year you visited, the colour was always there in much the same amount.

You drifted slowly though a flowery maze where there seemed little direction, passing a few features such as a small formal pond and under some more arches until at last you came to a small garden composed almost entirely of hardy geraniums. You may pause for a while and wonder why the garden's character has changed quite so dramatically, but there's no real mystery, it's simply that the garden's owner, in addition to making a large and beautifully stocked garden, also manages to find the time to run the national collection of geraniums, with all the organisation that this demands.
At the end of this last garden, having found your way thus far, there was a small hut and beyond that, a hole in the hedge. If you stepped through the hole you found yourself in a wide open space perhaps forty metres square. This area couldn't be more different from any of the others, being formally laid out with thousands of potted plants in neat rows. For in addition to the garden and the collection, the owner has also found the time to earn her living running a large and successful nursery. And no ordinary nursery either, because here you'd find a truly big range of plants, all well grown and cared for, many of them rare or at least difficult to obtain. It was easy to be tempted into buying a lot of plants, so good was the collection on offer, and you'd then pile them in a little heap by the shed while the owner added up the prices for you.
Having paid for them, you'd then suddenly realise that you had a considerable problem, because the only way to get your plants out of the nursery was to trail them back all the way through the garden along the little winding gravel paths, with no more than a small trolley at best to help you. It is a considerable compliment to the quality of the nursery that large numbers of people were prepared to do so, for you'd hardly ever be there alone, even outside of the high season. Yet the only explanation that I could ever find for the obvious lack of planning, if not to say the eccentric layout of the site, was that the gardener in charge had always been simply too busy to give any time or thought to such a thing as planning. This almost certainly must be the explanation since it fits so well with everything else that I know about her.

**

One special day in the late morning I called in for a visit which, for once, had nothing to do with plants. Having wandered through the garden and into the nursery I soon found the owner in her usual place, bent over with her head down in among the rows of potted plants. When I called out she popped up with her usual cheery smile and the beautiful but sunburned face that keen lady gardeners always seem to sport. It's a strange custom in our culture that men generally only ever seem to find the time for hats when they're working, and women only ever seem to wear them for leisure activities.

"Hello," she said, "you've come to see the trap, have you? This way!" She led me to a small wooden shed, the small available space inside almost filled with a giant contraption that looked rather like a large satellite dish. We dragged it out into the open and I helped her set it up. She then proceeded to dismantle it carefully and with obvious pleasure. Inside were a number of large flat reflective surfaces and at the centre, a huge and strangely formed electric light bulb, while beneath it were further chambers filled with cardboard egg trays and other seeming rubbish.

The device was, of course, a moth trap, and when it was set up at night in the garden with the light turned on, moths were attracted to it and drawn in. When once the moth had entered the trap, they naturally tended to find their way down into the egg tray area below where they were happy to remain until inspected, sitting through the daylight hours.

The nursery owner carefully removed the layers of cardboard and we looked down at several of the captured moths, including a beautiful Plume Moth, with wings like fine eiderdown, white and delicately cut, and several more subtly camouflaged to resemble lichen and bark, as though the whole natural environment had been copied onto little bits of paper by a skillful painter, and had been given life and set flying.

She explained that, after capture, the moths can then be photographed if needed, and are eventually released unharmed to go about their business. The records of the moths and other insects caught are then meticulously entered up into a detailed list, for this moth trapping is not done for personal amusement, although the lady undoubtedly enjoys the work enormously; there is in fact a serious purpose to it. The nurseries owner is part of the county recording scheme which endeavours to keep records of the ever-changing animal and plant populations of the county. Over time, she'd collected an enormous number of records, including her own personal statistics through which we browsed with interest for some time, trying to discern the underlying patterns in the trends.

I left eventually, having bought a few more plants, of course! But most of all I left wondering how one person could ever hope to fit so much in – running a garden, a nursery (with mail order) a national collection, two large, fit and well-walked dogs, her own home – and still find time for serious natural history. I suppose that if you enjoy it you find the time, or maybe it is just another instance of ‘if you want something doing, give it to a busy person’.

Only A Rose

At a very basic level there are only three common wild roses in Britain, the best known being the Dog Rose, Rosa canina. So well known and familiar is it that many people just use the name Dog Rose for any of the wild roses. However much can be added to the pleasures of the country if you're aware at the very least of the difference between the true Dog Rose, and the second commonest type, the Field Rose, Rosa arvensis.

Generally speaking they're not too difficult to separate, even at a glance (though there may be intermediate types) because generally speaking the Dog Rose, *Rosa canina,* has single pink flowers that are sometimes nearly (but rarely) completely white, whereas the Field Rose's, *Rosa arvensis*, flowers are almost always completely white, having a much larger tuft of bright yellow stamens at the flower's centre, large enough to be perhaps the most handsome feature of the flower, like a rich golden sun at the heart of the blossom. It also has a tendency, unlike the Dog Rose, to gather its flowers in bunches. Those characteristics alone should enable you to tell the two apart easily, and together form what a friend of mine calls the 'forty mile per hour characters' which you can spot, with a little practice, as you drive past in a car.

If, however, you should be lucky enough to get within a nose length of the plants, then you can add a couple more distinguishing features. The first is the fact that, in easy to remember terms, 'dogs smell'. Ah, sorry, let me put it another way – the flower of the Dog Rose is usually scented, while the Field Rose has no scent. Now, while my favourite collie bitch might be offended at that, it does make the dog-roses' first characteristic easy to remember.

The second characteristic is quite strange, and not easy to forget either, because dogs also have whiskers: to put that another way, the sepals of the Dog Rose – the leaves which cover the unopened bud and form a ring below the open flowers when open – have quite distinct and rather peculiarly frilled or whiskery edges to them. If you look really carefully you'll see that two of the five sepals have large irregular bristles on their edges, while strangely two of the others do not, but what is even more strange is that the fifth sepal is bristly on one side and plain on the other.

The sepals of the Field Rose, however, are only slightly roughened, which not only gives you a way to tell the plants apart when they're in flower but those characters will still persist even when the flowers have withered and the sepals are just brown scales on the end of the hips. The Field Rose is, incidentally, much less bristly in general, as both the teeth on the leaves and the thorns are much smaller and less spiky, which makes you wonder if the whole character of the plants, spiky or not, are perhaps determined by a single gene or gene complex which affects the whole plant from top to toe. No doubt that in a few years the genome of the roses will be unravelled and we may know for certain but until then it's merely a pretty speculation.

The one other rose that's fairly common, though not quite as widespread as the other two, and is also easy to distinguish, is the Eglantine of the poets, otherwise known as the Sweet Briar, or *Rosa elganteria*. You can tell the Elgantine easily by its extreme thorniness, with thorns of two types, both straight and hooked, growing thickly on its stems. An easy diagnostic feature that can quickly be confirmed is by bruising slightly and smelling its scented leaves, the fragrant character of which gives it the name of Sweet Briar.

There's also the Scottish or Burnet Rose to be found, as well as several others, some sub groups and various hybrids or crosses, all of which can give the specialist great scope for pursuing an enthusiasm, but are far from compulsory knowledge that everyone should have. For my own pleasure to date I've found that a little knowledge of the first two and perhaps the third, is enough to start with, if you only wish to add a smidgeon of pleasure to your country strolls.

Moorhens

Some years ago, having an idle moment and a tractor with driver to hand, I had a small pond dug just a short distance from the house. No sooner was this done than we were almost immediately adopted by a pair of moorhens who came and started to nest there within less than a couple of months of the pond being filled, and they or their inheritors have been there ever since – a total of some fourteen years now at least. I don't know if it's still the same pair who were here from the very beginning, as moorhens are very difficult to tell apart but it's a real possibility, since the most of the books on ornithology I've consulted tell me that moorhens have quite long lifespans.

It would be hard to count just how many hours of pleasure they've given me, or since the garden is often open to the public, how many people have enjoyed watching them. Nor have I yet met anyone with at least a degree of sensitivity who does not find these magical little rails completely engaging. They seem to captivate people totally with their subtle beauty, charming habits and most of all their comically big feet and white painted sterns. Especially well captivated is one lady member of the bowling club who often pops through the hole in the hedge from the bowling green next door to feed them, and then gives me a detailed report on how many chicks she's seen, their habits and rates of growth.

It wouldn't be surprising, however, to find that the books were wrong about how long the moorhen lives, as our particular pair seem to be exceptions to most of the rules that the books lay down. To begin with, they don't seem to be as shy and timid as they're sometimes described in certain literature. This could, of course, simply be because they've become well accustomed to humans by the constant traffic past the pond. They're certainly much shyer in the winter when there are fewer people about and they are not kept constantly busy with earnest nest building. In February when they're often out feeding on the bowling green, it only requires that I should appear at the end of the path some sixty yards away and they'll run for the cover of the far hedge. But in summer when they're busy on the pond and someone is walking past at least every hour of the day, they'll often do no more than move a couple of yards away and let out a warning 'poot' with little or no serious intent, even if I pass them by within a metre of the pond.

As you might expect, though, they're always much shyer when

caught on land than they are when you surprise them on the water. If, on my way down the garden in the early morning at the time when they're most likely to be straying away from the pond, I encounter one on a path, even at a distance of twenty or more yards, it immediately runs at great speed for the deepest cover it can find, often sounding a 'poot'. Though with a wonderful show of good sense it usually only does this after it's well out of sight.

This doesn't apply, however, when they have chicks, especially the very young ones, for then they become extremely cautious, and whenever anyone appears, an earnest scurrying takes place to marshal all the chicks into the cover of the pond's far bank, though sometimes it goes further and I'm warned off by a spread-winged head-down threat display from one of the birds. This particular form of shyness never seems to lessen no matter how many times a day I may walk past. When bird books use the word 'timid', it must surely depend entirely on your interpretation of that imprecise word, since on one particular, very special day I was a little regrettably the cause of a truly marvellous show of bravado.

**

I'd seen a large weed growing among the flowers on the other side of the pond that had somehow escaped my attention. Not wishing to let the moment pass, (the best time to pull a weed is when you see it!), and quite forgetting that the moorhens plus their brood of chicks were likely to be about, I immediately tramped, heavy boots and all, round to the far side of the pond. This was too much for the birds because it brought me within a couple of feet of a chick hidden in the weeds.

The response was both rapid and quite surprising: one of the pair immediately flew straight at me, flapping and calling with open beak and feathers spread. Throwing itself forward to within a foot of my face, it landed at my feet, and then thinking that it had done a good job of showing me who the pond belonged to, fled rapidly back to the water, chivvying a chick before it. This seemed at the time to be a truly amazing display of bravery for a bird listed as shy, especially so, as a human must be just the sort of size and type of animal that would normally see a moorhen as a good meal.

**

Nor do the moorhens on my pond seem have read the part where the books tell them that they should be, as they say, 'solitary and jealously territorial, rarely tolerating any other bird in their area except for their mates'. In fact last year when they managed to raise two broods of chicks, their surviving chicks from the first brood continued to live on the pond for a long while after they reached what you might call in human terms, adolescence, and the second brood were hatched out and on the water. For a long time these chicks from the first brood remained on their birth pond, helping the adults to feed the chicks from the second brood. Since the pond is not large, this gave the whole scene an appearance of great industry, with sometimes as many as four birds at once all busily feeding chicks with small bites of pond weed, all within an area of thirty square yards or so.

I've read of this type of breeding behaviour, where several generations of birds remain together in order to rear a brood of chicks, but I couldn't find any reference to it taking place in moorhens. In all probability it's old news to better and more experienced bird watchers, since it would be surprising indeed if our moorhens were quite that unique, but it's just the sort of fact that can slip below an author's mental radar when they're trying to list the things that they really need to tell people about – often maybe, for no other reason than that they take it for granted. I doubt therefore that any of my observations of moorhens have been original but what is all important to me is that they are, at least, original to me, bringing with them all the joys of discovery, no less than if they had been quite new to the whole world. I can't wait for next year and another season of watching the poultry.

Moonwort

Our local group of the fern society has for some time now been conducting a survey of a little known fern called Moonwort. For those who don't know the plant, Moonwort (called Botrichium when it's in formal company), is not at all like a typical woodland fern. It's a very small plant with habits more like an alpine bulb than the typical fern, with each plant consisting of only one small lobbed leaf, plus a similar sized golden spike which bears its spores. The two separate parts of the mature fern arise together from the ground to a height of no more than a finger length at best. The fertile spike grows just in front of the leaf which wraps protectively around it when they first push through the soil, and the whole plant can hide very easily among the grasses and herbs, especially in the untidy old pastures where it likes to grow, all of which makes it a very challenging plant to find, even for those who know it's there and are looking for it. The survey is being conducted on the roadside verges within the borders of the North Yorkshire National Park and involves numbers of volunteers walking slowly along the roadsides looking through the grass and heather. Their job is made even more difficult by the plant's own strange habit of mainly growing in pastures that are regularly grazed by sheep, which is not good since these animals seem to find it extremely tasty and a favourite food, so that it's often nibbled off at ground level long before we can find it. Now you may be thinking that hunting for Moonwort doesn't sound very exciting but in fact it's provided me with some of the most interesting of all my, admittedly rare, days out. To explain why, let me tell you the story of one such day.

**

We met first by the roadside one sunny day in late spring, in a sheltered vale deep in the heart of the moors. First of all came the greeting of old friends, some of whom had travelled several hours to reach the venue, and then the welcoming of new initiates. That done, and when everyone was coated and booted, we move off to do our hunting, together in a group to begin with. This is so that the more experienced hunters can get back into practice and at the same time help the less knowledgeable by showing them the methods.

This essential preliminary passes a happy hour of joking, light chatter and discreet flirting by some of the group, an activity I think that is always at its best out in the fresh air and sunshine. During the hour we hardly move more than a couple of hundred yards but some dozens of plants are easily found in a number of places, and happily nearly everyone makes a discovery. Perhaps maybe all our best efforts can only in the end add the tiniest portion to the sum of human knowledge but nearly every minute brings to at least one of the group a truly new experience of some sort, perhaps of some flower or insect never seen before, and there's always someone present with the knowledge to explain some of the wider significance of our discoveries. Then we can all stand back and share in the joys of first knowledge.

And all the while, whenever we look up from our task, the moors bring back the older joys of rediscovery: some old familiar but long missed sound, the skylark's song, wind in the grass, or merely the artless and aimless-sounding conversations of the sheep. Soon, however, each of us must go off alone or in pairs, to survey a given stretch of grassland.

**

Today mine is a long straight length of verge that slopes gently southward for more than a mile across an open part of the moor. I park the car in the gravel layby that marks the beginning of my allotment. Having enjoyed an hour of pleasant society, most of the morning is still left to enjoy the pleasures of solitude. The task naturally involves a lot of slow walking and staring down among the grass blades, nose pointed at the ground. The verges of the moors are, however, more than enjoyably rich in interest even if no Moonwort is to be found. In the blending of grass and heather along the roadside, many small plants find a nesting place and at this time in spring many of them are in flower – thymes and little sedums especially. Grasshoppers are everywhere, and at one stage a grouse makes me jump by springing out with a sudden noise just a few feet away.

Next comes a small frog, bright and full of life, which hops along in front of me for some way. It has managed to find found a home right out here on the wide moor, far from water and the places where people go. It hops off into the heather, quickly disappearing among the tall plants. Then the thought comes to me that in its whole life out

here, I may be the only human that it ever sees, and the only human who ever sees it. Making that short minute a unique experience for both of us; a small creature has been enjoyed, appreciated and given a passing thought which would perhaps never have happened if the Moonwort had not been brought me here at just this day and time.
The next event is a passing squall of rain, lasting just a couple of minutes, but as cold and sharp as only rain on the open moor can be. I had looked up before it arrived to watch it coming in, sweeping like a grey besom across the moor. I pull on my jacket and hood and it passes harmlessly, apart from slightly damp legs. But I take a minute to watch it come and go, as I do with quite a lot of the other clouds, since people who spend time looking down earnestly into the grass naturally become much more aware of the sky, and the sky here on the flat plateau of the moor is a grand sight by any standards. Some of the best advice I think I ever read, which I believe originated from the philosopher Rudolf Steiner, was that you should always look up to note what the sky is doing a least once per day, making notes, drawings or photographs if you wish – anything that helps you maintain the discipline of sky watching, because in the end it is mainly the looking that matters.
Eventually I get to the end of the road, I turn round and head back without seeing a single Moonwort but now it's time for social enjoyment again. A warm inn, hot food and excited conversation bring yet another mood into a day of gentle contrasts. In the course of a conversation that ranges from housebuilding, through weather lore and metaphysics down to the best place to buy fish, we each pass on the news of our findings.
Everyone it seems has found some Botrichium, except me. The chairman tells me that I should have seen at least one small group which he knows well, and which grows in the layby where I parked. When, however, he describes the exact spot, I realise that I must have parked the car right on top of it. The chairman is not impressed with this as an excuse, and clearly thinks me a little feckless.
On the way home I stop for a second look but even with the most careful inspection of the area that our chairman described, I still find no Moonwort. At least this proves that I didn't miss anything, the numerous sheep having found it first.

**

But now we must come to the strangest thing of all concerning Moonwort, which is that of all the plants which are found native or naturalised in these islands, it is arguable that there isn't one which has attracted anything like so much legend and folklore as Moonwort has. It was, for example, long thought of as sacred to the deities of the moon for no more reason than a small crescent-shaped mark on its leaves. In folklore, the uses to which it could be put, especially by people of ill intent such as witches and thieves, were innumerable, since according to legend it was able to open locks merely by putting a leaf in the keyhole; it put people to sleep against their will and if it was strewn on the ground behind you, it could baffle pursuers by making the nails spring from boots and horseshoes.

It is strange that all of this rich cultural history is associated with a tiny and economically useless plant that is difficult in the extreme to find (even when you're well informed and looking for it) and is practically invisible to the vast majority of people. This must surely be a true measure of just how much closer in contact with their environment people were in the distant past. Even in the Middle Ages, when (according to some modern scholarship) nature was held in fear and contempt, people somehow managed to notice and value a plant which even skilled botanists today consider obscure and difficult to find.

The Old Manor

One of the greater joys of gardening has to be the way in which it seems to network so well, this simple craft reaches out fingers which seem to touch just about every part of the natural world, and human culture as well. It finds a common and often overlapping boundary not only with history and natural history but also with agriculture, architecture, geology, palaeontology, culinary practice, geography, forestry, philosophy, myth and folklore, to name only the few that spring to mind immediately. And to a certain extent for a butterfly mind like mine, which is permanently looking for new boundaries to leap, this is what makes it such an ideal pursuit.

All gardeners take an interest in their plants that extends far beyond their mere physical presence, yet in most villages there are, I think, at least two types of gardener to be found. Firstly, there are those who have no interest beyond the parochial and who find that the main interest their plants give lies in the simple joys of remembering who it was first gave it to them or where they found it for sale, how many times they tried to grow it before at last they succeeded, if it once won them a prize at the garden club, and so on and so forth. There's no doubt that these are joys beyond measure, so much so that anyone who hasn't experienced them is to be pitied indeed. There is, however, another sort of gardener who I will call the 'bookish gardener', simply for want of a better name, though few of them would regard themselves as bookish in the usual sense of the word. In addition to all the other pleasures that plants can bring, these people bring a deep love of the history and romance that plants hold cupped in their petals. Many plants such as roses, herbs and trees have wonderful stories of past times that they can whisper in your ear every time you tour the garden, for no more than the price of exercising your imagination. In fact for some people this is often the main attraction of their plants. I should think that every village has a tree collector who loves to plant what he or she would no doubt call their 'grounds' with trees from all corners of the world, and for whom the dreams of far distant forests and the exotica of the timber trade are a good part of the pleasure to be had from them. Just as the tales of herb lore, which seem to completely bewitch the would-be earth mother that every village also seems to possess, bring a deeper shade of joy than the merely decorative flowers she tends.

**

Often in my early youth, when work at the manor house was slack or there was a real need, I would be sent down to the manor farm to help out. An elderly widow lived at the farm in what was known as the Old Manor House; this was always a pleasure and just getting there seemed to be something special. It was approached down a long, tree-lined drive that led off from the village lane.

The entrance to the drive was not in any way ostentatious, just a plain and simple but well-made farm gate of white painted wood which would hardly be noticed by a casual passer-by, especially since it was nestled half-hidden between two huge and ancient horse chestnuts. These, however, were not just ordinary chestnuts but a choice flowering form and in early summer their huge candles of flowers roared with the sound of bees plundering nectar for all they were worth. Just to stand under them and listen seemed to be one of those fundamental, overwhelming sound experiences, like thunder or the sound of waves on the beach.

After passing the gate I would then walk the quarter mile of lane shaded by tall lime, ash and maple trees. To one side an old unimproved pasture dotted with a few trees stretched out like a mini-park. It was usually haunted by a few nosy young beef cattle, to whom the rare passer-by was enough of a novelty in that quiet lane to make them come to the hedge and watch intently as you passed. This field, which had perhaps once been the home field of the manor, continued on beyond the old house, wrapping itself round three sides of the building and its small garden. On the fourth side stood the still-working farmyard so that the old manor, though it had long since been replaced by the new and much larger Victorian manor house, still seemed to be nestled naturally at the centre of the working farm. It was built of brick with stone windows in its heavily bent and age-cracked walls, which still nonetheless supported a number of large climbing plants without any signs of imminent collapse.

Passing through the gate, the paths and small paved area that led to the front door were made of old bricks salvaged from now long demolished farm buildings that had, no doubt, once clung close to the old house in the days when space and light were less valued than today, and a shorter walk in the snow to feed the livestock was thought to be a far greater benefit. Even this demolition, however, all took place a long time ago, and by my time the bricks had already been lifted and reset several times as they cracked and settled with the years. Yet they must have been good bricks in their day, for many more of them had become worn hollow with time rather than cracked with the frost.

In those later days when I knew it, however, there were no longer enough good bricks to pave the whole area before the house so that they had to be artfully rearranged to form little flower beds which made up the space, along with some old stone troughs and a few seats. The beds were planted with a great collection of herbs, flowers, small shrubs and alpines that spilled untidily wherever they would, yet all of them known by name and history to the owner.

**

Inside, the house was cool and cave-like, in the way that old thick walled houses often are, the rooms' walls and the backs of the great stone arched fireplaces painted white to make the interior seem bright and cheerful. The black beams, however, were hung with drying herbs which gave their scent to the whole house, but that was not by any means the full extent of the elderly widow's botanical collections. The window sills and the unused corners of the fireplaces were decorated with many vegetable curios, including strangely shaped pieces of tree roots found in the local wood and the large dried seed pods of Banksias and other Australian plants fetched back on visits to relatives on the other side of the world. And all of it told stories to the elderly widow. For not only was every plant in the garden known by name, where it was from, and from whom, she also knew the botanic and alternate names – often in several languages – and the histories of all the herbs and plant souvenirs within the house, with their common uses both domestic and medicinal. Yet the widow was no sentimental revivalist delving into cottage economics and herb lore while buying her plants and her know-how from the garden centre. She lived as she was brought up to live; all the plants formed part of her own history, most coming as gifts from other gardeners, and there seemed to her no difference between that and her book learning, belonging as she did to a last generation who saw such things as the natural accomplishments of good education.

For there was in the village at that time when I first remember it, a last few cottage gardens still remaining that were gardened quite unselfconsciously in the true vernacular tradition, a tradition which has now almost disappeared. Cottages who grew both roses and pigs in their gardens, not because they thought that these things would put them in touch with the earth, but simply because that was what everyone had always done.

Yet the widow at least proved that the two ways of seeing a plant were not mutually exclusive but could quite happily live together in one and the same person.

Heather

Usually just after mid summer each year I have to pay a visit to the moors of Yorkshire. This is mainly for business but I always try to find an interesting route back over the high moors with a little time to spare if possible. A few precious moments can then be snatched to stop by the roadside and have a meeting with some of the local plants. There are many little valleys and hollows in the moors that are worth a visit, not just the great and well known valleys and dales but some of the little dimples and dents in the moor, where rills too small to have names cross under the road by a narrow pipe and then carry on their way. Often there's a small lawn of sheep-mown turf to be seen, as fine as any bowling green, and a Rowan tree growing healthy and strong here in the high bright upland air, not filled with canker like those so often seen in lowland gardens.
There will usually also be some plants of Oreopteris limbosperma, the Lemon Scented or Mountain Fern, growing down by the water's edge and tucked in between the heather. Bright foliaged, pale lemon in colour, and a familiar sight to anyone who walks the hills, it's a truly lovely plant which well deserves its two English names. I always think, though, that it should be the colour that earns it its lemon name rather than the scent, because the citrus smell it's supposed to possess eludes my nose altogether, (friends tell me this is because I am dull and insensitive).
But the plant which dominates the whole scene is, of course, the heather and if I'm lucky enough, my late summer visit to the moors will correspond with the height of its flowering; wave after wave of purple, both as uniform and as varied as the sea. This surely should be considered one of the natural wonders of the world, no less than the famously ephemeral flowering bursts that occur when rain occasionally falls on the water-starved deserts of the sub-tropics, though in some ways a wetter more rain-washed desert is exactly what moors are.
If you've been hanging out with plants for a while, you might easily think that there are two kinds of plants in the world, those that appeal to gardeners and those that are favoured by the botanists – and there is of course some truth in this. Yet it's not quite so simple as all that. Why? Because I suspect from what I know of most gardeners that they are explorers by nature and forever wanting to widen their horizons, always in search of the next new plant or an up-to-the-minute growing method. I also suspect that most of all they

frequently look over the garden fence and wonder if the world of plants beyond their borders – the plants that are better known to the botanist and naturalist – have anything of interest to offer. For most gardeners there's much interest to be found in the wider realms of plant lore; the road is clear if you can only put the hoe down long enough and take the time to look over the fence, and especially if you're not put off too much by the more esoteric edges of botany.

**

Take the heathers as an example. Most people, even non-gardeners would I think be able to identify a heather on sight, and most people possess at least a basic understanding of heather ecology, even if they don't generally realise that they do. By that I simply mean, they understand that heathers are the characteristic and definitive plants of heathland, even if they don't spot the dead giveaway clue in the habitat's name. What's more, in all probability they have at least an intuitive understanding that heathland is generally found on the margins and in the wilder and less cultivated parts of Britain. It's also possible that quite a lot of people would guess that these wilder places beyond the edge of the ploughed lands are traditionally kept as heath mainly because the soil is poor and thin, or high and sloping. And just before we give up on this list of possibles, I suspect that many people can perhaps remember that deliberate burning is used in many places to maintain the heaths in good order and prevent the spread of trees.

Now when you add all that up, you'll realise that you actually knew quite a bit of botany and ecology all along without even being aware of it. So why not let's try pushing our mutual knowledge just one step further, with some information that's probably just a little less a part of common everyday currency.

I would guess that one thing that most people are unaware of is that there are not one but six or more main groups of heathers or heaths found wild in Britain of which two, namely the true Heather, also known as Ling or Calluna, and the Bell Heathers, otherwise known as Heaths or Erica, stand out. This multiplicity of types is almost certainly not widespread knowledge among the public at large but I would make an estimate that most keen gardeners would have the beginnings of an inkling of this, especially if they've ever bought heathers for the garden. They will then have learned that the Erica are generally the winter flowering heathers which will grow on most

soils including the chalk, while the Calluna are summer flowering and require that you should check that your soil contains no lime or chalk, since they need a acid soil.
We've reached point where we're now stood firmly with our backs to the garden fence, having reached the outer limit of the common heather lore that is in everyday use by large numbers of people. Yet if you're with me so far and haven't given up in boredom at venturing into such realms of exotica, let's really push the boat out and adventure way beyond the safety that you'll find on a garden centre label.

**

Calluna is almost certainly the most important of the wild heathers and most moorlands are composed chiefly of this tall and impressive species. It's the one that forms most of the great swaths of purple that I look for on my trips to Yorkshire, growing strongly on any of the peaty or sandy soils where Rhododendrons and the like thrive. Calluna, or Ling in English, can easily be distinguished from the other heaths found in Britain by the fact that its leaves take the form of wide scales which cling to the side of the stems, making the stems appear almost like fuzzy leaves themselves. The Erica, on the other hand, has needle-like leaves which stick out from the stems in whorls, much more like the shoots of conifers. And that's all there is to this little smidgeon of botany.
Yet now that you know this, the moors and heaths suddenly have all the more meaning. The Calluna becomes an old friend while the Erica, whenever you see them since they are less common, though not rare, become something distinguished from the common sort. With time you may even begin to put together an informal impression of the heathland ecology of your local area, all of this coming with just the tiniest bit of botanic knowledge. The point being that to learn botany may often seem daunting to the gardener: As one famously said, "I want to learn about plants but I won't learn botany". But of course you don't have to learn botany, certainly not all of it. You can learn just little bits, picking here and there as you choose, and which will enhance your experience and enjoyment no end.

Hellebores

The older I grow the less sure I am that I really know anything – nature especially seems to play so many tricks. A perfect example of this occurred to me as I was touring my garden one spring and admiring the fine show that the hellebores were giving. As I did so, I was reminded of one of the commonest pieces of gardening wisdom, handed down to the point of banality, that oriental hellebores will stop flowering if they aren't lifted and divided every few years. Yet I sometimes wonder if it is so.

I know from experience that great benefits will follow if you lift and divide many perennials and I would never have found any reason to disagree with this idea, had I not done some work in the garden of a very wise and experienced older gardener called Mrs Moor. She showed me round her garden one afternoon when the work was finished, filled as it was with huge clumps of hellebores flowering powerfully, and she explained that they hadn't been divided for many years. I didn't of course immediately assume that it would be possible for everyone to grow such superb hellebores without ever dividing them. After all, there are too many variables of climate, soil and shade at work, and I know well enough that a method of doing anything which works for one person in one garden is not necessarily going to work in lot of other gardens, especially not in mine.

**

Some years later, however, I branched out into the nursery trade, and for several years I was extremely busy developing the new business, which meant that the pleasure garden had to endure much neglect at precisely the time of year when hellebores are best divided. The result was that since they hadn't been divided for a couple of years anyway the hellebores went undivided for some five or six years in all. Eventually there was a little more time available and it became possible to divide them but when I looked at them they were still full of flower, and I must say that the large bold clumps made a far stronger statement than is usual with the smaller clumps that result from splitting.

Remembering Mrs Moor's experience, I therefore decided to try growing them on as an experiment, without further cultivation.

Eventually some fifteen years passed and still they showed no signs of decline, though my conditions are perhaps in many ways ideal for hellebores, so it may not work everywhere. I could, however, believe that Mrs Moor's theory was proved, at least for a minimum of two very different gardens. But then in the winter of 2008 I finally noticed a small reduction in the number of flowers on each clump, and eventually in the winter of 2009, the hellebores failed to flower much at all.

So at this point I made the decision that they would have to be lifted and divided after all, and that Mrs Moors' theory was finally proved wrong. Unfortunately, or perhaps fortunately, circumstances once more prevented me from getting into the garden. This proved to be a piece of really good fortune because despite being given no care at all, the hellebores flowered wonderfully well again in 2010, with flowers in numbers and of sizes I'd never seen before. Whatever the reason that they failed to flower the year before, whether they needed to rest or if some freak trick of the climate made them unhappy, I will perhaps never know but it would seem that whatever the reason, it had nothing to do with the clumps being undivided.

It is of, course, a common fallacy among gardeners that happy plants should be in full flower every year. In truth many, wild plants especially, are cyclical in flowering and often have rest years. For some – like the common and familiar beech tree, which famously according to a not-quite-accurate legend, only sets seed one year in four; or bracken which some people say only makes spore one year in ten – this is perfectly natural and doesn't indicate that the plant is in anyway unhealthy.

A gardener's response to a mature plant failing to flower is (being human), to assume something's wrong, and in the absence of any signs of disease the plant gets divided. Inevitably the following year it flowers well, as naturally it would after giving itself a rest but the result is, of course, assumed to be the direct result of our intervention. It's only too human to assume that when good things happen it is a justified reward for our wonderful virtues!

It's far too easy to make errors based on too limited a range of experience in the garden. For years now I've happily shown visitors to our garden a beautiful mature bay laurel and assured them that the bay was quite hardy in this county based on experience with this plant alone, and assured them also that the trick was to plant a large mature specimen in the first place, since it is young small plants that are really vulnerable. Until that is, the very severe winter of 2010,

following which, as you may guess, our very mature bay upped and died.
All of which means that for ten years I've been handing out advice about the hardiness of some shrubs which is quite wrong; for many years I would have told you that you needed to divide hellebores, for several I would have told you that you didn't need to after all, then for one year I would have said that, 'yes you probably should,' and now I don't even agree with that any longer.

**

I once remember having a spare patch of rough ground which was cleared and cultivated but for which I had no particular use. I decided to sow and try to naturalise some wild flower seed. This was back in the days long before the fashion for meadow gardens became widespread, so there were no ready made mixtures available and you had to source each type of seed separately and mix them yourself. In the first year after sowing the mixture it looked very fine indeed. The second year it still looked well, though I felt there was perhaps a bit much toadflax in the mixture. I kept it gently weeded, however, respecting most of the flowers that were in the original sowing but by the third year the toadflax was becoming quite dominant. By the fourth there remained little else but a sea of creamy yellow toadflax.
A few years later when meadow and wildflower planting were beginning to become fashionable, I entered into conversation with a lady of great experience both as a gardener and also in her full-time profession as a botanist, who expressed scepticism about the whole meadow-planting scheme. She said that it was very unlikely ever to work as people intended because almost invariably one species would come to dominate and you would never, at least on a small to medium scale, achieve a balanced mixed ecology. I thought back to my toadflax border and agreed that in my limited experience that what she said was true.
But then on my way home I came to think about it more deeply and I remembered that I was far from being disappointed with the toadflax border. It was on the whole quite a spectacle and never failed to delight or attract comments from visitors. And so, though in essence the wild flower border had failed, there was now something bright and gorgeous that it could well be argued was even more special and worthwhile as a garden ornament than my intended meadow,

and it had been achieved almost completely by accident.

Wild flower meadows are supposed to be reflections of nature, and it's true that you can often find highly mixed meadows and prairies in nature, where many different species live in balance. But it's also true that nature sometimes produces a complete monoculture where just one species dominates. Nature is, in short, nothing if not diverse in its diversity. And who is there among us has not marvelled at a pasture in the high dales stained bright golden yellow with buttercups, or a purple heather moor, a copse filled with bluebells or a field red with poppies – single flowers all of them. So that if, despite your best efforts, your attempts at naturalisation fail to produce exactly what you visualised in the first place, does it matter? Or have you gained something that is all your own and maybe better, plus a little lesson in practical ecology?

Which only leaves me to say that in the end all I've learned for certain in gardening is that the best thing you can do is simply to try it for yourself, use the minimum of intervention if you're brave enough, and see what happens. And most of all, that it's best not to take any advice about gardening, especially not from people like me.

Growing your own

This village is forced, like most villages I suppose, to organise a number of fund raising events each year in order to cover some of its necessary (and often not so necessary) expenses. This usually involves the same small number of the willing and worthy people who organise such things, stretching their imagination annually to constantly produce a string of new and novel events, all of which are designed to lure people from the comfort of their homes and make them part with some of their hard-earned money. Race Nights have always been popular, these events showing films of old horse races projected onto the wall of the village hall, in which the names of the horses have been changed just in case anyone should remember the race, and then getting people to bet money on them.

On the whole, given that they're a great chance to share food, drink and gossip with everyone, these events were quite a pleasant way to spend an evening. Some compensation, I suppose, since I've never really seen the amusement in gambling, and second-hand horse racing seems to be a pointless way of spending an evening, yet support the village we must, so there I sat...

Between races, however, I get talking to Paul who's staying with relatives while he thinks of moving into the village permanently. He's hoping to grow vegetables in his new garden but wonders if it's really worth trying since all his previous efforts have failed badly. I ask him what he'd tried and he gives me a short list of seeds, acquired presumably from a garden centre. Some of these are things that should be easy to grow but several could be quite challenging, and no one seems to have given him any advice as to the best things with which to start.

I would have liked to have given him a short list of really easy bombproof plants which provide plenty of dietary interest and are guaranteed to get even the most inexperienced of beginners off to a good start, no matter what – hopefully in time encouraging them to try their hand at harder challenges. A beginner in any field should be given a few easy successes to start with so that they aren't discouraged, and this is especially important in any hobby pursuit where they've no need to continue if it doesn't seem to promise any rewards. Yet this sort of advice often seems hard to come by, partly I think because even gardeners are sadly not immune from the common failing of wanting to retain their mystique by making their

craft seem harder than it really is.
So for Paul and anyone else like him who may want it, here's my list of the 'so easy they're almost foolproof' ways to grow a lot of food, and give any good cook the sort of opportunities that only super-abundant fresh produce can.

**

The first thing that almost every beginner seems to start with are potatoes – maybe because they're always assumed to be a staple and therefore the natural beginning. True, but then again, it would be hard to pick a plant which was more difficult to grow! Potatoes require challenging cultivation, including a degree of blanching called earthing-up, they're martyrs to more pests and diseases than perhaps any other garden plant, and are bulky and difficult to store. It's surely crushing to anyone having their first go at growing to have their whole crop eaten by slugs or rotted by blight; that sort of thing can kill a beginner's interest at the start.
Not only that but the rewards are few; very good potatoes raised by professional farmers who have both the know-how and the equipment to do it well, can be bought very cheaply and easily from supermarket or farm shop. All of which means that the 'spud' has probably been responsible for putting more people off 'growing your own' than any other plant in the vegetable plot. If you do grow any at all, it's best to grow just the early or new potatoes since these are more expensive in the shops, they benefit from being eaten as fresh as possible, (run up the garden!), and come early enough to escape most of the pests and diseases.
But fortunately there are many plants that are not only much easier but also much more rewarding to grow than potatoes. Almost certainly the easiest vegetables to grow – and things which can be expensive in the shops relative to the difficulty of growing them and the space they occupy – are salad crops. The non-hearting types of lettuce such 'cos' and many of the oriental salads such as 'matzuma' are easy to sow and they germinate quickly, require little aftercare, have few pests and last a long time for your efforts because you just cut what you want, then they'll simply grow back again.
Spring onions too are easy to sow and grow, while nothing could be easier to grow than radish – so much so that many gardeners sow these as marker crops, sowing them along the rows where other crops have been sown; the radishes will come through quickly

showing where the other slower seeds are to follow. It's true that radish and most salad crops suffer from slugs sometimes but you can generally get round this by harvesting them first and cutting away the damage. If it gets too bad you can just scrap the remaining crop and plant something else. The seeds of these salad crops are rarely expensive but the benefits of a free super-abundance of fresh salad – and what could you want really fresh if not a salad – really change your ways in the kitchen.

**

The legumes, or peas and beans, are among the easiest of all the larger vegetables, and also the most decorative for those without a patch dedicated to vegetables alone. With very few pests and large seeds which are easy to sow and germinate readily, they have few problems, save only the small and obvious one, that most of them require some support such as sticks or canes to climb up. However, you're under no obligation to make a neat job of this, any rough twigs or prunings will usually do, and if you only grow the dwarf French beans then you needn't even bother with those, though nothing could be more handsome, even in the flower border, than a well trained row of runner beans. Other than providing support, all you need do is to drop the seeds in the ground at around 30cm (1ft) distance apart and at the depth given on the packet.

Few seeds are more satisfying to grow than legumes. Peas and beans are what seeds should be – vigorous and thrusting, big and bright when they first come through, they give the sort of pleasing experience that is exactly what you hope for when you sow seeds. One tip that's worth passing on about legumes is that the more you pick them the more you get, so start pulling them as young and tender as you can, and be prepared to give some away. You can also eat the new shoots of peas, so you don't even have to grow them to maturity to get a crop.

Carrots and onions are a little more challenging because although the seeds are easy to start, they do require some aftercare and are prone to some pests and diseases. The worst of these can be guarded against by planting the two of them close together because the flies which are the worst pests of both are put off by the scent of each other's plants; this is one piece of old lore which really does work. The best way to avoid problems is to harvest them both early, as 'baby' vegetables, before the problems start, which you can easily do when you're growing your own. You can also sow your seeds closer and enjoy the thinnings.

**

Perhaps the easiest things to start with of all are some of the perennial herbs. Not all of them are easy because the plants called herbs aren't really a true botanical group but just a ragbag collection of plants people find useful, and they therefore contain many things which grow like weeds – some that are in fact common weeds – and also some things which are really difficult. It's all about choice.
Many beginners would, I suspect, choose to start with parsley but I think this is a mistake since parsley is anything but easy to grow. Experienced gardeners often forget how things that seem easy and obvious to them may seem very difficult to the totally inexperienced. My first choice of herbs would instead be chives. Buy a pot and plant it out in spring or get a friend to let you dig some up – you don't even have to bother with seeds. Then just forget it, and if the soil around it is not overworked or overweeded it will sow itself and spread naturally.
Chives only ask for a little sun and that they aren't planted in a bog, which are probably the only facts that you need to know about growing most herbs successfully; most of the common ones need some sun and won't therefore grow in full shade, and that's about as technical as it gets. Chives especially are also good value for the space they take, since you don't need many to impart an onion flavour to salads and sandwiches, or even for cooking.
Most of the onion family, to which chives belong, aren't too difficult to grow, so you can plant both onions and shallots without worry. The easy way is by buying sets, which are small ready-made bulbs, from the seed merchant or garden centre. These, if planted just half way up the bulb, will soon fill out to full size without any extra care. The onions do have some problems but you can just throw bad ones away. They do need lifting, drying and storing in a dry place if you wish to keep them long term, but this isn't much to ask for things that are almost indispensable to any cook.
Then comes the big three herbs, rosemary, thyme and sage. It would be hard for any cook to do without these three, and they couldn't be easier to grow, given that they need just the same conditions as the chives, a little sun and a soil which isn't sopping wet, though if your land floods in the winter then I'm afraid you'll

have to build them a raised bed or grow them in containers. But the really good thing about this little trinity is that they're all (including the low growing thyme) plants of the type which gardeners call woody shrubs, which means that they're no harder to grow than any ornamental shrub or hedge – you just plant them in a hole and water for a few weeks if it's a dry summer when you plant. They need no feeding and normally suffer no diseases. They may in some ways be easier than most shrubs because the cutting you do for the kitchen means they need a little less clipping or pruning; just give them time before you start cutting hard.

There are at least two other herbs which are also easy, if you only have the space because they're quite big. And these are lovage and fennel. Both of these are big tall growing plants, non-invasive, give good value in a mixed flower border, are problem free and therefore give exceptionally good value. The only problem with fennel (we are talking about the leafy herb here and not the root vegetable) is that the two are easily confused. But plants of the leaf form can easily be bought at any herb nursery, and they should know the difference. While the uses of fennel in cooking, in fish dishes, sauces and on barbecues are too well known to need describing here, lovage may be more of a mystery. Enough to say that it's a celery-flavoured leaf herb which finds a use in a wide range of savoury dishes. And what should be said about both is that the shop bought form is not remotely an equal of the fresh plant from the garden.

If however you have a damp and shady garden that simply won't grow any of these herbs, don't despair because there are a couple of plants for which damp and shade are fine, though both are tolerant enough to take some sun and drought. The first is mint, one of the few herbs that relish damp and shade. There can, however, be a couple of problems with mint, one of which is that if it likes its spot then it can be quite vigorous and invasive. The usual advice given about this is to grow it in a container but mint is rarely happy in a tub unless it's a really big one, and in any case there are a number of mints to choose from, some of which, if you take the advice of a herb specialist, aren't too bad. Much better therefore to choose one of these and plant your mint in a rough corner where it can do no harm. The other slight problem with mint is that it really needs a little feeding to keep it truly happy, but it isn't a picky feeder and any old compost, manure or leaf mould thrown at it every year or two will do. And I mean thrown – just sprinkled over all of it or dumped over part of it will do, and there's no need to dig in.

The same goes for the other moist, shady, corner-loving herb, namely rhubarb, which really is a herb though it's more often thought of as a fruit or a vegetable. But certainly, apart from throwing it a little garden waste now and again, nothing could be easier to grow. It doesn't even need moisture or shade really but just does a little better there. If you do want a job, though, you can lift and divide it now and again and it will benefit, but it will grow forever even without that effort if you just throw some organic rubbish over it in winter which is the sort of feeding it likes – lawn-mowings, spent potting compost, kitchen waste and even good garden compost will all do. You can buy it as roots ready to plant, and if you manage to grow a lot and wish to try something considered quite advanced (but which is in fact quite easy) then you can try forcing it. To do this all you need do is to put a large lightproof container, for example a bucket, over part of it in spring before it comes up, and you'll then get early tender sweet shoots. Don't do it too long and move the bucket each year to a new place; you'll soon come to understand the niceties with experience.

**

Which brings us to fruit. Perhaps the most difficult of all fruit to produce well has to be the ever-popular strawberries with their need for annual renewal, protection from a wide range of pests, the difficulties of weeding them, and keeping them from rotting all contributing to make them one of the neediest plants you can grow. It could not therefore be more ironic that the wild or alpine strawberries, which are exactly the same thing but unimproved by breeding, are perhaps the easiest of all fruit that you could attempt. You simply plant them in any bit of clear ground – they don't mind shade, and they romp around forming the most perfect natural ground cover you could ask for. It's true that in really tidy gardens they may be just a little too vigorous but if you aren't a control freak then they're just fine, forming neat compact eight-inch high plants. They hold their fruit and very pretty white flowers up above the ground (and most pests) on nice elegant stems which need no extra support and which make them easy to pick. It's true that the fruits are tiny but they have a luxurious flavour, can be used for everything that the larger fruit are used for and they require no more effort than just the picking.

They also provide just the perfect weed-suppressing, root-cooling, soil-protecting 'green' mulch that many larger plants revel in, so they actually save you effort. The only down side is that they can be hard to find in nurseries and garden centres: you may find them under Fragaria, though even then you have to beware the purely ornamental flowering types, but believe me they're well worth the hunt.

If you were to ask me what is the easiest of all the bush fruit to grow, then I'd say blackcurrants. It's true that they need some pruning but if you're not too fussy then this may be no more than cutting about half the stems – preferably the older ones – back to the base each year; they can be given more clever pruning but they'll do fine with no more than that. It's also true that they have one or two pest and diseases of which 'big bud' is perhaps the commonest, but these are rarely very harmful, and 'big bud' is easily diagnosed since it makes the bush produce large round cabbage-shaped leaf buds, just like it says on the tin, and the best treatment is just to cut them out. Of tree fruit, I consider plums to be perhaps the easiest and certainly one of the most versatile for the kitchen.

There are no doubt many more plants you can grow for food which are just as easy and rewarding as these few but they'll do well enough to get anyone started, whatever their tastes in food and there's nothing like a little early success to make a person want to be more adventurous and try some real challenges. So maybe the list is not merely an invitation to be timid but just the opposite – a sound starting block from which you may launch to who knows where!

Ground Cover

Fashion moves slowly in gardening – quite literally and for obvious reasons, a little slower than plants grow; and as always it's the things which were at the height of fashion the last time the pendulum swung that are now at the very bottom. One of the big swings in recent years has been the way that ground cover has acquired such a bad name after being the idol of the garden retail trade just a few years ago, because unfortunately it became far too deeply involved with the oxymoron fashion called 'maintenance free gardening'. Consequently, many of the perfectly good plants used for it have fallen out of fashion too.

No one thing has the answer to all problems in any field, and people who are looking for easy gardens are sadly, also usually, looking for easy answers. When the maintenance-free hokum was at its height, people were told that weeding could be eliminated by ground cover plants in vast numbers 'smothering' the weeds. There is, as far as I know, no plant that grows fast enough to smother weeds, at least not one that can restrain itself from strangling all other plants or swamping a nice wide path as soon as your back's turned. Did anyone ever see a weed being smothered, anyway? I don't know about you, but the weeds in my garden are made of far sterner stuff than that!

Yet having said that, (and as always in gardening), I think it's rarely a good thing to reject any idea out of hand, however banal it may seem when viewed through the stained lens of dated fashion. For every technique that can be used in a garden there are, almost certainly at least, a few places in every garden for which nothing else will do quite so well. Just as there is always a place for even the most 'out-of-fashion' plant.

**

It would be sad to miss some of the benefits of a useful technique altogether, and there are real benefits, make no mistake. To begin with, many of the best shaped plants, those sometimes referred to as 'architectural', often look by far their best when growing free of all other competitors so that their shape can be seen to full advantage. This, however, can lead to a rather bald garden if we only keep the soil around them weeded to bareness. If we really want borders and beds to have the maximum of interest, it's best to avoid putting too many plants of the same shape and size together. If we do this we can end up with a nice cushiony well-upholstered garden, but without much shape or drama.

So it naturally follows that if we're to get the biggest possible range of contrasts into our gardens, we should find space for something low and flat, as well as the upright and the bulky. I prefer to think of 'carpeters' rather than ground cover. As well as a bonus to the aesthetic gains, there's a real cultural benefit because most of the bigger plants gain immeasurably from having their feet down among the 'green mulch'. In my garden it's easy to see which plants have the advantage of ground cover round their roots by the appearance they give of sheer enjoyment in life. If you doubt it, just come and lift a bit of my creeping Woodruff and you'll see, even in warmest days of high summer, just how cool, moist and humus-rich it is down there; you could happily push your nose into it and take a big sniff. And if it suits your nose, just think what a lovely place it would be to go if you were a fibrous root tip!

Most of these benefits are lost, however, if you do use too many of the genuine big, coarse so-called weed 'smotherers' which all too soon turn into garden stranglers, and which is maybe the reason why ground cover gardening earned itself a bad name in the first place. Some of my favourites are plants such as the common native Woodruff already mentioned. I just can't get enough of it. Nothing could look as fresh as it does in the spring, covered as it is with pristine white flowers, looking just as though a little bit of the wild woods floor had been lifted up and dropped into the garden.

A carpet of Woodruff, Asperula odorata, in any shady spot is a pure delight. True, you don't get the benefit of its scent in the garden in any meaningful way, (For that you have to dry it.) but it is in many ways the ideal carpeter, strong enough to look after itself but modest enough to give no offence to larger, if not necessarily more important plants. This seems to me to be just about as big and bold as a plant can get and still fill the role of good carpeting. Some people will say that even Woodruff is coarse and invasive but how many plants do most of us grow that will be threatened by a plant rarely more than ankle high?

If Woodruff does have any weakness it is that of bearing far too close a resemblance, when not in flower at least, to that little horror, the common cleavers (or goosegrass, sticky willow, call it what you will). Constant vigilance is therefore needed to see that the clinging little monster doesn't infiltrate itself among the Woodruff. You couldn't, therefore, call it maintenance free gardening. No, there is in fact, just enough work to keep your inner puritan quite happy if you wish. But for this you get a garden bed which has the mood of a wild native copse in the spring, and untangling the odd cleaver is surely much more satisfying than mindlessly pushing the hoe through bare soil.

There are many reasons why some perfectly good and beautiful plants are rarely grown, languishing in the dark back kitchens of life when they should be out on display at the heart of every garden. Some, no doubt, have acquired a bad reputation, perhaps because of some small failing which may only occur in a limited range of special situations. Others have fallen from fashion, and some maybe, aren't loved by nurseries because they're difficult in pots or hard to propagate.

**

Perhaps one of the saddest reasons, however, must be the true Cinderella complex, plants that are overshadowed by much bigger, coarser, pushier and unlovely relatives. One such is the Yellow Pimpernel, forever in the shadow of its pushier and regrettably very similarly named relative, Creeping Jenny, (Lysimachia nemorum and L. nummularia). Yellow Pimpernel, however, is a really very refined form of Creeping Jenny, with a much more modest stature, more finely pointed leaves and delicately shapely flowers. Moreover if you choose to give it a home, you'll be helping along a moderately uncommon British native. For me it's the perfect ground cover, forming a fine delicate carpet of fresh green, against which plants of a taller stature stand out proudly, and all of this with the bonus of fine starry yellow flowers through the summer.

More of a second choice is one of the many small creeping Sedums, including the red leaved forms. They only make second place because, though reliable and evergreen, they are to my mind just a little coarse. This doesn't matter in some places but I wouldn't, for example, like to see delicate spring bulbs pushing though them as I would with the first two, since that would just seem inappropriate. I do find, however, that they're surprisingly tolerant of shade for things that are usually listed with alpines; they can even be used beneath trees and ferns with no ill effects.

Wild strawberries also find a welcome home with me. I know that some people will consider these to be just too big, bold and aggressive for their gardens, and I would only use them myself in the wilder corners of semi-neglect. Certainly they wouldn't suit small neat beds but then again, that just means that the beds should have been made bigger in the first place! Regrettably, wild strawberries don't fruit well if you plant them in shade, which is the main area I like to use them. But they still make a perfect green quilt beneath the trees, and a few fruits make a nice bonus if you can bother to pick them. After all, one small wild strawberry is worth twenty cultivated ones, even if the latter are twenty times the size.

Pulmonarias and Ajugas also do well for me in this role but these plants are beginning to approach the size of ground cover which can no longer be called carpeting. But whatever is used, it is, I think, important to avoid using too many types of plants in any one place. This makes for a bitty, fractured and far too fussy-looking border, and is perhaps the other main reason that ground cover gets a bad name. Whatever is used for a carpet, it is best that a carpet should be truly that – a plain textured background to all the other plantings. At least, that is, where it is not to be the main feature. You may after all, have a mosaic on your floor but if you do, it would pay to keep the furniture to a minimum. But that's another story.

Playing Gooseberry

It often seems strange how people can sometimes become involved in a certain thing to such an extent that they begin to seem eccentric to many people. How can people spend hours obsessively pursuing the idea, for example, of some perfect dahlia, just for a few hours' display on the show bench? The short answer is, of course, that we should be grateful that they do, whatever their motivations, for the life of everyone would be far duller if they all stopped. But there may well be more to it than this.

And I have a tale of gooseberries to tell. The problem of the gooseberries started innocently enough, with the need to find a use for the bare ground in the old orchard. Soft fruit seemed to be the natural choice and so, just as an experiment to begin with, the rhubarb patch was transplanted and enlarged to fill one corner. The next stage was to buy six blackcurrant and ten gooseberry bushes, the initial idea simply being to provide soft fruit for the house, and perhaps a little for sale.

At first all went well, the bushes and the rhubarb grew well and were soon yielding a good crop of fruit – nearly all, in fact, that we could wish to use. The real trouble, however, was that they only filled about a fifth of the available area, and there was a great deal of space left over, but fortunately both blackcurrants and gooseberries are easy to propagate from cuttings and so I doubled their numbers quite quickly. Consequently it wasn't very long before I was the proud possessor of no less than twenty-two bushes, all neatly ranged out in straight rows, and since I was then very young and quite enthusiastic about everything, each bush was inevitably pruned to the highest standard of textbook perfection.

It was that perfection, however, that really started to cause the problems because the bushes not only gave us quite a lot of fruit but they looked good as well. In fact, to my eyes there was little else that looked quite as fine as those perfectly straight rows of neatly pruned bushes, but because they were so well pruned and cared for they yielded fruit of quite exceptional size and quality, all of which naturally helped to swell my pride in them. Not vanity, you understand, but genuine pride, for one thing was certain – nobody except me ever went into the old orchard, let alone admired the gooseberries.

It wasn't so much the blackcurrants, for though blackcurrants are quite good-looking plants which need only a modest amount of skill to prune them well, they are by no means in the same class as a gooseberry bush. A well-pruned gooseberry, on the other hand, is quite a small work of art, requiring a lot more skill to prune it well than almost any soft fruit, and when so treated it looks a perfect little star. For a gooseberry stands proud on a short leg, and when pruned to perfection the branches can be made to sweep elegantly upwards, and all of them at exactly the same angle.

The sun must also be considered in a well-pruned gooseberry, for the fruit mustn't be shaded by too much foliage or it won't grow and ripen well and in bad cases, may develop mildew and other fungal diseases. The bushes must also be kept strictly within bounds so that they don't brush one another and can still be picked, while the ground beneath should ideally be kept immaculately clean. The result of all this is that a properly cared for gooseberry orchard is a thing of exceptional neatness, with row after row of perfectly symmetrical inverted leafy funnels each standing on a little leg, and every bush nearly as tweaked and fussed over as any bonsai on a show bench.

Naturally as I gained experience in all of this, I became ever more pleased with myself, and began to think that nothing would look quite so pleasing as filling the whole orchard with gooseberries. Maybe we could even sell some of the fruit as well. It never occurred to me that there may not be a big market for gooseberries in a small isolated village. Gooseberries are, as I said, easy to root from cuttings, and it always seemed a shame just to throw away all the prunings. It didn't take long, therefore, before I'd filled the whole orchard and eventually had a hundred and fifty bushes, all standing proud in seven straight lines. It's strange how young men think that straightness is almost a moral virtue.

As you may imagine it took hours to pick them, and even longer to prune them. But I didn't mind – quite the contrary, to my mind that was all part of the joy of it, the longer I could spend indulging in the task of pruning the better, and the more time I spent with the bushes the more I doted on them.

Ultimately the problem came with the fruit, for two or three years down the line the bushes were yielding huge quantities. In the end, however, even I was forced to admit that we had more gooseberries than we could ever hope to use. After all, there is something to be said even for strawberry jam, especially when you haven't tasted it for years. The gooseberries eventually became an embarrassment. I couldn't sell them or give them away, there was only so much wine you could drink and so much jam you could make. I really needed to dig up and dispose of some of the surplice.

I was, however, relieved of the need to dig up any of my beloved gooseberries because it happened that shortly after we moved house and like it or not I had to leave the gooseberry bushes behind. The most disappointing thing about the move was, however, the strict ultimatum that came with the new garden. "Absolutely no gooseberries under any circumstances." But at least one good thing came out of my brief gooseberry obsession which is that I can now understand and admire the deep obsession that many people have with their hobbies much better than I ever did before. I'm at least cured of it myself. Maybe even for good.

Which just leaves me with one niggling doubt, which is just the slight feeling that – thinking back – it may just be possible that somewhere, lying so deep that it could never be admitted, we may just have moved house in order to escape the gooseberries...

Other People's Gardens

Our village has for many years now held various annual garden competitions, awarding prizes to those gardens that are judged to be the best. This usually provides me with the pleasant job of escorting several members of our own or sometimes another village's garden club, on a pleasant morning stroll round the village viewing its gardens, retreating eventually to the shelter of the tearooms for refreshment, debate and planning. What makes it even better is that usually the walk is held in high summer, when the swifts circle high in the air above the village square, so that the guide has always something to watch when he's not wanted: we're very lucky in this village in many ways, and we've rarely been troubled by bad weather.

Over the years the format of the contest has been changed many times, as it has always been difficult to suit all needs. These days we have to be content with judging front gardens only, since getting people to volunteer their gardens so that we may judge the backs as well has always proved difficult. Sadly the reason for this seems to be the widely held belief that a small number of gardens are predestined to win, and it's not therefore really worth anyone else's time entering. This is however completely mistaken and doubly sad, because if there is one thing that I've learned over the years, it's the almost complete impossibility of predicting the judges' choice. Over the years individual judges have picked a huge range of gardens, often for a quite eccentric range of reasons, which means that almost any garden may win. The other thing that I've learned when escorting the judges, is that truly knowledgeable and experienced gardeners rarely judge the efforts of others with anything but kindness and appreciation, and that no garden can be found which does not win some admiration.

Of course no one, least of all me, ever achieves perfection or even achieves their best work all the time, which is part of the fun and challenge of it, and why it's a good idea that we are forgiving whenever we regard the efforts of fellow gardeners – if their efforts are well intentioned, that is. Nothing makes me more angry than garden snobbery, or those who sneer at the efforts of others simply because the results do not match their own personal ideas of taste. I find this especially irritating when those who suffer the sneering have clearly expended real effort in their gardening and in many cases, have shown as much appreciation of the contents, (which is the truly important thing) as those who sneer. A garden is the personal space of its creator, for their enjoyment and the enhancement of their lives alone, even more so in some ways than their houses where enjoyment compromises with many other uses besides; and if a garden only serves that purpose, then it has achieved much.

Yet having said all of that, it still makes me very sad when people fail with their gardens. Not perhaps through lack of taste or resources, but chiefly when they fail through lack of effort or want of caring. In the end there's a responsibility which underlies all gardening, a moral base as absolute and as grim as the underlying bedrock. For when we garden we take on the care of a piece of the earth, which is almost certainly the most precious and finite of all the commodities we can possibly possess.

**

Please let me tell you a story.

Not long ago an experiment was undertaken in England. Several acres of land which until that time had always been under the plough, and which had never seen any natural growth for many generations, were set aside with a fence around them, and they were then left completely untouched, excepting for occasional visits by the experimenters themselves to see what would happen. It was thought at the beginning that if the land was left for long enough, then something that resembled natural forest would eventually grow back.

That is what happened, but what really surprised the academics at the college where this experiment took place, was the speed with which the forest returned. In twenty or thirty years from the start there was already a near complete covering of trees, and in only fifty years or so, to the complete surprise of the experimenters, something which most people would very easily have mistaken for original natural forest had returned to fill the site.

I've never visited that woodland myself, never walked under the shade of its boughs or felt the leaves underfoot. I don't however think I need to, because I know with confidence even without ever seeing it, that all of it is beautiful. Moreover, I know that there is almost nobody alive who will not agree that they find it beautiful, and all of this achieved just by simple neglect and a tiny amount of

patience.
It is a story that should be of interest to most people but especially gardeners, because at the very least, it demonstrates just what nature can do in a very short time and without any help at all.
Please don't misunderstand, this isn't in any way implied as a criticism of gardening in general. Our gardens in this country are a vast nature reserve anyway, and one which costs the neither the taxpayer nor wildlife charities a penny. The idea of the 'wild garden' is of course a completely false one – you can never truly recreate a wild habit in a garden but the important thing is you don't need to. The perception that there exists a difference between artificial and natural is a human one. The blackbird and the fox don't make any such distinction – to them all that matters is that it serves their purposes.
Though of course the question still has to be asked, at least of those who garden. If you take a really honest and critical look at your garden, then can you in all frankness say that it is truly as beautiful, and that it makes as great a contribution to the wider environment as that unseen wood does? There are, I've no doubt, a lucky few of us who can say yes it is, and it does, but for most of us, including myself, then the answer I think is most probably no. There's nothing wrong with that because gardening needs to be a matter of many compromises, a broad church, and few of us have the space for a wild wood anyway. Yet this land that we are privileged to garden is not only precious and irreplaceable but capable of doing and being so much. Do we not truly fail therefore, not only if we fail to labour hard enough, but much more importantly, if we fail to enjoy and appreciate it as much as our limitations allow?

Forgotten

One year we had some visitors who were really keen to collect some sloes to cook with but unfortunately it was a poor year for sloes, and it being quite late, most of the roadside bushes had been picked clean. The fashion for sloe gin has in recent years put a plant – which in my youth was a forgotten and neglected wilding – at a premium. People therefore rush out into the local lanes to pick them as soon as they're half ripe, hoping to grab their share before everyone else gets to them. This is a shame because sloes are one of those fruits which reach their peak only after they've had a frost on the bush, the vast majority often now being picked before they're ready – not a good thing for the discerning cook who wants the best that they can offer.

Nor are they hard to find in the hedgerow since, if you have your wits about you, the white blackthorn flowers are easily visible in the spring as one of the earliest and most spectacular of the season's flowering displays. You have only therefore to note where the flowers appear in spring, then go back in the autumn to collect the fruits.

It's interesting to note that local people often refer not only to the fruits as sloes but also use the same name for the bushes on which they grow. In the spring, however, those same people call the bushes blackthorn. This means that the same plants have one name in the autumn when they're wanted for their fruit, and another in spring when they're admired for their flowers. Perhaps it would be best to stick with Prunus spinosa which at least tells you that the blackthorn is a relative of the plums and damsons with which it can sometimes be confused. A problem even more likely to occur as it can hybridise with damsons, and sometimes the sweetest wild sloes are in fact damson crosses.

The flowers are small and arranged close to the stems, as if they're clustering close to avoid the cold, which they may well be doing, because the blackthorn is one of the earliest shrubs to flower, putting out its flowers in March when the weather is often at its worst. Everything about the blackthorn seems to send a draught of cold down your spine, from the stark black twigs to the cold white flowers, the sight of which would make a snowflake shiver, and the acid bite of the raw fruit which seems to set your teeth on edge instantly.

Many country people in this area still believe in the legend of the blackthorn winter, saying that the flowering of the blackthorn always brings on a period of late cold weather with frost and snow, though as early as March there are so many cold snaps it's almost certain that one is bound to overlap with the thorn's long flowering period.

**

Deep in our local woods there's a long straight forest track. It's not part of the way marked tourist routes, and the first part looks quite dull so that few people go down it. It is, by Lincolnshire standards, a long walk but it leads eventually to one of the quietest and most tranquil arms of the forest where it sticks out into the surrounding farmland. Neglected by tourists and ramblers but still full of interest, it's there that you can often watch the deer and foxes going about their business in a perfectly natural way, with little thought that humans may be nearby.

I knew that there were some large blackthorn bushes that often cropped well, hidden in that quiet part of the woods and I was sure they wouldn't have been found by casual pickers. So I suggested a walk to my visitors and they were enthused by the idea, so we set off in search of them. Regrettably one of the visitors was not as fit as I thought and found the walk more than a little too much but at least the sloes were there, so I didn't have to face the embarrassment of trailing them a long way through the woods to no avail.

The crop couldn't have been much better since there were several large bushes standing close together in a line and they faced a small clearing in the woods so that they got plenty of light for growth and ripening fruit. My visitors were delighted to find such huge bushes, untrimmed for years by hedge cutters, and to get all they wanted in just one place. These were quite exceptional bushes, much more like true standard fruit trees than the hedgerow bushes of the roadside; clearly here they had been thriving on neglect and had reverted to their true nature with enthusiasm.

You would wonder how it was that such a common plant of open places, hedgerows and lanes could have found itself in the deep forest in the first place, and especially why it was never completely smothered by the conifers or removed by the foresters. Yet the fact that the bushes grew in a straight line was a plain clue because it was obvious that they'd once formed part of a hedgerow, probably growing in the open beside a lane or track on what was once

farmland.
The Forestry Commission had obviously taken advantage of the established lane and used it for their own trackway, hence the little bit of open space and light which still reached the forest floor at that point. But it had all been too much for the usual hawthorns, dog roses and elders which are the blackthorns' normal partners, having plainly given up the fight against the conifers' ever-deepening shade long ago, so that not a trace of them remained. Clearly the blackthorn is good at withstanding shade and competition from tree roots.

**

There are, however, a few other survivors from the past that help to fill in the story with even more detail, one of which is an old apple tree in the hedgerow at the forest's edge perhaps thirty metres away, which hints that perhaps there had been some human habitation nearby with maybe an orchard not far from the house. But the real giveaway is just a few yards further back into the woods behind the blackthorns because there the usual ground flora of brambles and ferns which you find everywhere throughout the forest is replaced by a large stand of nettles several metres square. Something is obviously different about this part of the woodland floor and it's not hard to guess what, because nettles are usually found in the wild only where there has been human activity and more often than not human habitation in the past.
The reason is that two things encourage nettles; one is grazing by livestock which tend to nibble away the nettles' competitors but tend not to favour eating nettles. The other is the presence of high nutrient levels in the soil, especially nitrogen and phosphate, both of which are usually found in artificially high concentrations only where humans have been active, concentrating the livestock in small areas and dumping their waste and animal manure. The nitrogen is only moderately persistent in the soil and rarely in short supply but phosphate is always at a premium in nature and an increase in phosphate levels can affect the ground for years. In the true wild, you also usually only find stands of nettles near to water courses, ponds and other such places because the other thing that they require is a little moisture. That is rare in the deep woods, especially on this light sandy soil beneath the conifers, so it's doubly certain that there's something unusual here.

**

One quiet day on my own, I explored the nettle stands behind the blackthorns and kicking away the moss I found, as expected, the remains of old crumbling bricks and old fashioned lime mortar in the last stages of decay, confirming that there had once been human habitation here. It also showed where the nettles find their extra bit of moisture, inserting their roots down into the cool root runs between the old foundations. But the truth is that it hardly needs bricks and mortar to show that there must have been a farm there once. The plants themselves are enough for that, persisting like living fossil traces long after the living farm has vanished.

And the ghostly presence of plants can persist for a very long time indeed, renewing themselves for generations but never giving up their foothold on a site long after the buildings and all traces of human habitation are gone. Some stands of nettles are known to have grown on the sites of long vanished medieval castles and villages for centuries, and yet there are none just a few metres away in the farmland despite the belief that they spread rapidly.

But perhaps one of the best of all the indicator plants is ironically the ground elder, Aegopodium podagraria, an apparently common weed which is considered by many gardeners as the worst curse nature can inflict on you. It is a low growing spreading perennial with bipinate leaves, very like those of the elder from which it gets its common name, though the resemblance is only coincidental since the two plants are not remotely related. In the garden it spreads rapidly by long thin underground runners which can push their way through the root balls of larger plants and beneath paving. It can regrow even if the smallest piece of the runner is left behind after an attempt to dig it out, and in real terms it is therefore almost impossible to control without resort to weedkillers.

The surprising thing, however, is that for a plant which is a major pest to householders and gardeners in towns and villages, it has very little impact as a weed on farmland, and only occasionally in true wilderness. The reason for this is that the ground elder rarely flowers and hardly ever sets seed in Britain; instead it relies on spreading entirely by its underground runners, so that every clump in a village lane, garden or under the churchyard fence is just one plant which has spread there from somewhere nearby. Indeed, in the average village most of the clumps will have spread from just one or two original plants, moving from garden to garden through the hedges and under the walls. Sometimes it will have had a little help: as gardeners in the past exchanged and traded manure, plants or topsoil, it only needed one small root to be present in a plant's root ball or in a barrow load of compost, and another garden would be infected. Yet this only applied to gardens and waste spaces around villages because ground elder is not a native plant, and originally it simply didn't exist in the wider countryside.

It was probably introduced in the first place by the Romans, who ate it and grew it as a pot herb used for its strong leafy flavour. It's hard to imagine, though it must be true, that today's terrible weed which many gardeners curse, must once have crossed the channel on board a ship in a well tended plant pot, carefully placed in the hold or strapped to the deck and fretted over by its watchful owner. An owner who no doubt was already trying to imagine how much the plants would fetch in the market place, finding an easy sale to new colonists eager for the comforts of home, in a new land across the water.

The church and the monasteries then continued to propagate it throughout the Middle Ages, especially because it was valued as a cure for gout, which gained its other common names of 'gout weed' and 'bishop weed'. No doubt much of the benefit that was gained came, as it was from many of the medieval herbs, simply from the addition of fresh green stuff to the diets of the rich.

But the ground elder lingered long after the monasteries were dissolved and the rich took to pills from the doctor and pharmacy. So that today it is still found in the older towns and villages, often still close to the churchyard, the village centre or where it can haunt the ruins of the castle and the abbey, giving away by its presence the sites of older habitation. Its role as an indicator of human occupation probably will not last much longer in the modern world, though. The motor car, which has changed nearly every part of human life, has brought into being the modern custom of fly tipping, so that the ground elder is slowly here and there, in lay-bys, car parks and field gates, beginning to find itself out in the wider countryside, in places where nobody ever gardened.

**

The philosopher Socrates said that, "There is truth in wine and children," meaning that drunkenness, and the innocent gossiping of our offspring will often betray our true thoughts and intentions no matter how carefully we may dissemble when sober and childless. Plants, however, are also given to betray our activities in a similar fashion, often showing to the skilled reader of a landscape what took place before, and what is to be found below.

According to myth just such a betrayal of human presence was once spotted by the native Americans who were highly skilled in reading the landscape. The plant in question was the common plantain, the small familiar weed of lawns and flowerbeds, which has a rosette of flat pointed leaves lying on the ground, and the rather attractive brown flowering spikes which rise to twenty centimetres or so. The plantain was quite rare in America until recent times, so that the Native Americans noticed when and where it first appeared, giving it the imaginative name of 'white man's footprint'. This is probably because, being a weed of ploughed agricultural land managed in the European style, and having no doubt adapted over the centuries to just that lifestyle, it seemed to follow the immigrant colonists wherever they went, lingering even when their fields were fallow or abandoned.

And the reverse is also true, sometimes the green survivors can tell you not only what people did in the past but also what they took away. A stand of bracken and heather in the hedgerow and the verge, even glimpsed swiftly from a passing car, betray that the country you are passing through was once heathland. A moor that was perhaps removed generations ago but which now still lingers as a tiny ghostly remnant, even when there are only ploughed fields beyond the hedge.

It is not just the archaeologist who can use crop marks viewed from the air to show what people may have done in the past. The nettle, the apple tree in the wood and the bracken by the roadside can tell all of us, even the most pedestrian, (especially the pedestrian) about our local history and what happened to the land as people moved over it, if we only pay attention. The plants are completely frank, tell no lies, and betray our every significant act, if we only will listen to their stories.

A Little Old Fashioned Formality

A big part (and some of the most fun parts) of a nursery's year are the country fairs and shows we visit to promote our plants and services. Generally we sell quite a few plants at most of them, though we tend to think that the publicity we gain is much more important to us than the revenue from the plants sold. In many cases, though, the main benefit is just the simple pleasure of getting out to interesting locations and having the excuse to visit beautiful gardens and houses, especially in the season when work at the nursery is generally too intense and preoccupying for holidays.

One day we were attending a fair at Doddington Hall, a sixteenth century house of very grand proportions, rustically set in deep wooded countryside, yet still in plain sight of Lincoln's distant hilltop cathedral. The nurseries which book stalls at the fair are usually put in the formal garden between the hall itself and the gatehouse. A large rectangular space enclosed by walls and marked out within into several smaller enclosures by low clipped box hedges. There are a few shrubs around the walls, a gravel drive and some paths, but little more. If you enter down the main drive, you first pass under a wide gate arch and then emerge into the sun as the ancient and heavy wooden gate clunks closed behind you. You can then see the elegant patterns of the garden that form an almost perfect frame for the architecture of the house which, I have no doubt, was the original designer's intent.

To many modern eyes the garden would seem to be a feature of almost austere, if not puritanical formality, even though it almost certainly reflects just the sort of garden which would have been there when the house was first built (though I of course have no real evidence for that). Indeed, for all I know there could have been almost anything in the space but it's just the right sort of area for this form of garden; and if not, then what was here originally may well have been an even plainer courtyard, or perhaps merely a simple carriage drive.

In fact something like that is almost certainly just the style you would expect for a house of the period. Yet in some ways does it not seem a little odd? After all the house itself is in the Tudor style, at a time when fashion was fast evolving towards the Baroque, with domes on the roof, heraldry over the door, many windows and stone ornamentation on the corners. Designers at that time were certainly not afraid of decoration in architecture. Why then should gardens be, as they often seem to our eyes, austere?

**

Within an hour of our arrival at the hall, and once we had put out our plant selling paraphernalia – the plants, the sales table and cloths, the signs, leaflets for giving away plus the large umbrella which shades our table – I went off and parked the van with still a little time to go before the opening. Looking round it seemed that everyone else, perhaps twenty nurseries or so, had done the same, creating as they did so an almost unnaturally colourful vista which seemed well worth a photograph. So I stepped back against the side walls with the camera and began to frame the scene.

And it was at that point that I remembered an old piece of garden lore I'd heard long ago, about gardens before the nineteenth century being designed primarily so that they could be decorated, not by flowers or any of the products of horticulture, but by the visitors and other people who moved through them. The idea was that in Tudor, Stuart and Georgian times, when people – especially the rich – wore large volumes of elaborate clothing, it was the householders and visitors themselves who formed the main decorative elements in the gardens. This would be particularly so on the high days and holidays, for which the gardens of the time were mainly managed, when the paths and gravel areas would all be filled with people parading in their best holiday finery.

There's no doubt there's a lot of truth in this idea, but just think of the practical issues, too. It doesn't take much effort to imagine a time when women wore hoops beneath their skirts, and men's dress included thigh boots and swords which stuck out three feet to the side. Then, as you may guess, people who resembled galleons in full sail needed a lot of room just to manoeuvre. It was not an age of swift motion.

It was also an age when many houses contained long galleries, special rooms provided for little other reason than to give the upper classes space enough to walk and parade when the weather outside was inclement – just walking being an important pastime in the time before almost any form of commercial entertainment. So important was space in order for the well dressed to circulate that both the furniture (and the servants!) were usually made to stand against the walls; even the huge dining tables were routinely moved to the sides by groups of servants after meals had been eaten. There would in any case have been much less furniture. Much of what we see in the really old houses today is the accumulation of the centuries; before the nineteenth century furnishings of all kinds were rare and houses invariably sparse.

These sorts of habits no doubt extended to the gardens as well, and of course even when the gardens were not wanted for the aristocrats' use, those many servants hurrying about their business would still have filled the outdoor rooms with lots of life and labour. It may be true that the term, 'outdoor rooms' was invented in the 1970s by fashionable garden designers but the idea of them I think was not. These formal spaces were originally made plain and austere – not for puritanical reasons of taste but because they were intended to be filled with people in times when people and community were the main assets that most estates, even the wealthiest, possessed. For the open countryside beyond was a lonely bandit-haunted place, so that the numerous servants and tenants represented not merely comfort, but financial and physical safety as well.

It is I think a mistake to see this supposed austerity as a sign that there once existed a golden age when tastes were more refined and plain than today's degenerate and vulgar manners; for the one thing that these gardens were not originally intended to be about was any form of minimalist and puritanical good taste. Such gardens were for show above all else, not only of the horticultural skills practiced on the limited plant materials then available but as frames for all the tailored wonders of fabric the country could muster; with silks and satins, gold braid, plumes, swords, fans, dresses built like marques and hats the size of parachutes; anything and everything in fact that would be named today with that useful modern term of 'bling'.

Yet maybe for just a short while on these new fashioned modern holidays, when the gardens are hosts to tourists, markets, fêtes and fairs, it is sometimes perhaps just possible, to stand back by a moss cooled wall and for a minute or two see a ghost of what once was. When these spaces today are crowded and filled with all the gaudy show modern commerce can put on display, you can perhaps just half close your eyes and see a faint vision of what once was intended in the days of high formality. Try it.

Flora

Occasionally I'm asked to help with the floral decorations in one or more of the local churches. Although not a regular myself, the privilege of decorating a fine old building for some pleasant holiday event is still a wonderful gift. Though I don't share the faith these institutions represent, I still have an appreciation of tradition, if only because it feels amazing to take part in such an old custom, because the association of flowers with reverence could not be more ancient.

It may well date back unbroken through the Middle Ages, to the garlanded pagan temples of ancient history, and even to the graves of the pre-human Neanderthals who covered the bodies of their dead with layers of flowers. It could indeed be the oldest tradition we have, and is certainly far older than any religious practices that yet exist. What else, except perhaps hunting, could we do that links our hands in sympathy with those of a Neanderthal? By comparison with that, any theology seems but a trite and temporary new imposter.

There is no doubt, though, that the English parish church could hardly be a better place to display flowers. The massive great walls are cool and humid enough to keep cut flowers perfectly fresh from one Sunday to the next, while the backlight of Gothic windows could have been designed to shine perfectly through delicate plant tissues. Even the Reformation did the country's florists a favour, if nothing else, when it gleefully stripped away the churches' decorations and replaced them with the chromatically neutral whitewash and empty niches beloved of the puritans.

And what an incredible range of opportunities the church year gives, from the rich, warm gaudiness of Christmas decorations, through the light, delicate pastel confections (favoured for spring weddings especially), to the vegetable extravagance of the harvest celebrations, even though these last are now sadly fading from the national psyche. And all of them I suspect, bring as much joy to their makers as they do to the congregations, (who probably view them as an alternative to being bored by clergymen).

Arranging flowers is one of the simple tasks which is always, at least if not taken too seriously, a joy, since not only are there all the rewards that come from working with natural materials and employing ourselves in handicrafts, but also because flower arranging is the most forgiving of crafts, since by using only the most natural of materials it's hard to make them look anything less than wonderful. Even the most inept of arrangers cannot help but make something beautiful with even the simplest of found twigs and home-grown garden flowers.

Yet having said that, there's still as much scope for talent to display its virtues as in any art – you need only go to your county flower show to see the amazing things that can be done with this medium. And yet, it's also there among the displays of high floral art and the grand themed exhibits which have absorbed the talents of whole teams for long hours, that you will see some of the least pleasing examples of the craft, because in truth these grand exhibits have come a long way from the simple decorations of church and home. In creating these 'masterpieces', I think they sometimes lose touch with their roots perhaps, in ways that make them less joyous even as their artistry rises.

The Japanese have a useful phrase, 'Wabi-Sabi' which means the beauty of rough, old, rustic, and especially temporary fading things, a property which I think cannot be separated from the best of floral art. Certainly the grand displays of flowers that you find at the shows seem to be an entirely different craft from the one used to decorate the dinner table, the hearth and the church window, and I wonder to what extent those floral skills carefully learned to win prizes in shows, are ever used in the home – any more than the prize vegetable growers' skills are ever used to grow something you can actually eat.

Sometimes in a church you do though, encounter something between the two. For example, at annual flower festivals used to raise money for church funds, where the arrangers are certainly trying to impress with their skills in order to persuade visitors to give generously. Yet they aren't competing for prizes, the overall effect of the display and not the demonstration of skill being the important thing.

**

Some years ago I was happily employed on a window for just such a festival. Our theme was 'The Plays of Shakespeare', and the luck of the draw meant that I was given The Merchant Of Venice to represent, which proved to be amusing if nothing else, with plenty of visual gimmicks to construct beforehand. This was a true show piece! You always doubt how it will turn out, of course, but that's where the forgiving nature of the flowers themselves comes in to play, for arranging is one of the few crafts where the end result always seems more pleasing than the vision you had of it at the start; unlike writing or most of the other visual arts, where the end result always seems to fall short of your original vision. Eventually when as you find yourself succeeding well, you soon forget your worries and start to lose yourself in the materials, the endlessly variable stems and leaves, the shapes and colours, and most of all, working in the cool quiet atmosphere of the church soon means your mind becomes empty of all but the task. Perhaps achieving that perfect state of self-forgetfulness which Buddhists believe is the most blissful state that a human can reach.

In the end the result turns out to be not too bad, and the local schoolteacher, (who seemed to be spending the day idling in the church for no apparent reason other than showing off his knowledge of the theme) seems well impressed with it, and makes many flattering comments. At least I've finally realised what it is that makes schoolteachers seem so peculiar when compared to the normal population. It must be obvious to some people but it has only just occurred to me that immaturity is, of course, an infectious condition. But what I wish is that I'd tried less hard to portray the theme and concentrated more on showing off the materials. An Elizabethan like Shakespeare himself who knew, 'A bank whereon the wild thyme blows, Where oxlips and the nodding violet grows, Quite over-canopied with luscious woodbine...' would have appreciated that. For in the end it is that forgiving quality of the natural plant materials that is all-important in making flower arrangement both a popular and a successful art, and I think that the same thing applies to at least the best sort of gardening.

**

Incidentally, it occurs to me that some people might ask why a self-confessed sceptic is doing the flowers in a church. Well, the answer to that is simply that in part it depends on a tolerant and friendly vicar, but much more on a belief in the village and the village community that trumps the disbelief in any religious doctrine. And if that sounds to you a little insincere or a case of trying to have your cake and eat it, then let me put it this way. I like sometimes, much more than anything, to take walks in the countryside, and one of the best things about this is to visit the many rural churches in this country.

Yet there is a dilemma in so doing because I feel that, having enjoyed the historic building, its art and its architecture, it is incumbent on me to place something in the collection box in order to contribute to the building's upkeep. However I know that this donation can never really be ring-fenced just for use in the maintenance of the fabric, and that some of it will go towards the promotion of a belief system that I do not share. One solution therefore is to make only half the contribution that I feel a believer would, though in practise this cannot be ring-fenced either, and I know that my gesture is in reality just silly. But some moral dilemmas are insoluble, and at least being reminded of the need for some moral ambiguity in an honest life is a guard against dogma and the belief in absolutes, which really should be left entirely with the faithful.

History of Ferns

The human heritage associated with ferns is extremely rich, perhaps richer than any group of plants except for the culinary and medicinal herbs, which is saying a lot for plants which can be so easily overlooked in the modern rush. I can only provide here a potted account of fern history and lore, while hoping that you'll be inspired to delve further, for if you're at all like me, then I'm sure that you'll feel that a great deal is added to the pleasures of growing ferns by the rich romance of their almost limitless history.

One of the first things that happened when humans began to change the landscape was that the Spleenworts, or members of the Asplenium genus of small pretty alpine ferns, began to find that things were changing to their advantage, and they're probably more common in the artificial environment of walls than ever they were on natural rocks and cliffs. They found that the artificial cliffs and rock faces made by humans suited them very well, perhaps even better than their wild habitat, so that as soon as people started to build walls they began to thrive and prosper as never before, being among the commonest of wall plants.

Early on in their history, humans soon began to make use of ferns, especially for medicine, so that the Spleenworts were able to repay their debt to us – since at least classical times – for building all those walls. The genus Asplenium gets its name from the use of one of its former members, Asplenium ceterach, now Ceterach officinalis, to treat diseases which involved enlargement of the spleen, apparently a common symptom in the fever-ridden ancient world. Indeed so potent was A. ceterach believed to be that it was thought a large enough dose could make the spleen shrivel and disappear completely.

However, perhaps the most common uses of ferns in ancient herbalism was as a vermifuge – that is, for the purpose of expelling intestinal worms, possession of which seems to have been a common ailment in the past judging by the sheer number of plants employed for this purpose. It must also have been considered a very serious ailment for such desperate cures, as many of the ferns used, such as Polypodiums and our common British native Male Fern, Dryopteris filix-mas, are thought in modern medical opinion to be

highly poisonous.
Fortunately the Male Fern at least did find other more attractive herbal uses, and from medieval times onwards, was the principle source of the 'fern' scents that are extracted from its ground rhizome. The fragrance is present to a lesser degree in the Male Ferns fronds, and also in the foliage of a few other ferns such as the fronds of Gymnocarpium robertianum, the Limestone Polypod. It could, however, be a challenge to obtain the benefits of these scents in the garden, as they are of the elusive bushed leaf type, readily available to the nurseryman with a tray of plants on the potting bench but much less obvious outdoors. Male Fern had perhaps the widest range of herbal uses found for any fern, some of which would hardly be passed by a modern clinical trial, and being regarded in folklore as a powerful love potion among other things!
It seems also that according to folklore, Male Fern was the main source of the so-called 'fern seed' which, it was supposed, had the power to make people invisible. This idea may have arisen because, as most people know, ferns don't have flowers or seeds. However, to the medieval mind it seemed logical to presume that all plants must have seeds. Therefore, (and probably how this idea may have arisen) since no one had ever seen a fern seed, it was concluded that the seeds themselves must be invisible, and so naturally had the ability to pass on this property. Fern seed could never have been very popular or widely used though because, if mythology is to be believed, it was only shed at midnight on Midsummer's night, and then only to people who had gone through a series of elaborate and dangerous rituals to prepare themselves beforehand.

**

The value of ferns in the past was, however, by no means limited to the herbal and mythical, nor to their obvious uses for such things as animal bedding and insulation. For in the days when every natural resource was necessarily husbanded thriftily, numerous economic values were found in ferns. Bracken fronds, for example, were widely cut and burned to make the soda needed for glass and soap-making industries, and some kilns built for this purpose can still be seen in the Lake District where this was a major industry. At the same time (mainly in the east), Equisetums or Horsetails, the common wayside weeds that have a similar botany to ferns, were needed in such large amounts for polishing silverware and other small items in the cutlery and toy trades, that Britain was forced to import extra plants from Holland, under the name of Dutch Rush.

It isn't known if medieval people grew the ferns that they needed in their herb gardens or merely collected them when wanted from the wild. But it's certain that some ferns, though sadly not the wild natives, were highly regarded as garden plants by as early as the seventeenth century. Interest was stimulated greatly by many new introductions, mainly from the New World, which were brought in by plant hunters, such as the Tradascants. Many of these ferns, such as Adiantum pedatum, the Goosefoot Maidenhair – an interesting and quite tough garden plant with strange fronds resembling tattered umbrellas – were no doubt quite hardy in British gardens but little was known of them and, being regarded as exotica, most went into the orangeries and hot houses of the very rich. While all the time just over the garden walls, the British native ferns, a flora just as exciting if not quite as large as that of North America, was passed by without much regard.

That soon changed, however, for by the nineteenth century the natural sciences were the height of fashion, especially with the burgeoning middle classes, for whom a little dilettante botany was the ideal way to prove one's social credentials. The ferns as a plant group suited this mood perfectly and by high Victorian times ferns were by far the most fashionable plants, to be both admired in the wild and grown in the garden, taking over from the roses that had been all the rage in the first quarter of the nineteenth century, and being replaced by alpines and orchids in the later half.

Naturally, as most of these people couldn't afford to travel abroad, they turned to the native ferns to fulfill most of their needs. This may not have been good for the ferns themselves, since by the height of the so-called 'Fern Craze', thousands of Victorians were venturing out to the hills and lanes (aided by the new railways) and armed with specially made fern trowels in search of plants. If you didn't care to find your own ferns, you could employ the services of professional 'Fern Hunters' to do it for you – for a price, naturally. It was always the rarest that were most prized and collected, and they were almost certainly the quickest to die when they reached the cities; so sought after were they it is almost certainly the case that our fern flora has still not fully recovered to this day.

**

The craze was certainly fuelled by the new fashion for greenhouses, and Wardian cases, or terrariums (often in those days called Fern Cases) were by now becoming affordable for many people, and which, in theory at least, would enable you to grow even the difficult and tender Filmy Ferns in a cold dark and smoky city home.

The idea of the semi-sealed indoor cloche, or bottle garden, was first conceived accidentally by Dr Nathanial Ward after whom it was named, when he placed the chrysalis of a moth in a glass jar to hatch out, along with some soil to keep it moist. When he returned months later, he found that a fern had grown in the soil. This was a striking irony, as ferns were just the plants the doctor had been trying to grow without any success for years, in his cold, dark and highly polluted Victorian home. He then realised that plants, and ferns especially, would grow very well indeed in a nearly sealed glass container. At first the idea was taken up most quickly by plant hunters and shipping companies, as a way of shipping live plants overseas but soon Wardian cases and terrariums had become extravagantly elaborate pieces of furniture which graced the Victorian home, thereby further fuelling the demand for ferns, still often considered to this day by far the best plants for such situations.

By the middle of the century ferns were everywhere. You could literally fill your house with them, not just in pots and terrariums but even printed on your curtains, wallpaper and tablecloths. You could even see their images in the cast-iron brackets which held up the roofs of many public buildings. And of course there was only one group of plants that could conceivably be used as table decorations at the fashionably serious dinner party by any hosts with even the least pretensions.

But as you know, it always ends in tears, and as the new century approached, a reaction set in. Suddenly the ultra-fashionable became everything that was old fashioned. From being the most wanted of garden plants, ferns fell to being the most despised. As the word 'Victorian' began to become associated with words such as 'fusty' and 'fussy', so ferns began to be associated with everything that was unsatisfactory about the old styles of gardening; no one even wished to have them carved on to their coffin any longer!

There was however one good legacy. The Victorians' interest in the rare and unusual had driven them to collect all the monstrous and genetically deformed plants they could find – the greater the deviation from the natural species the better. And if you couldn't find the extreme, then you could indulge in ever longer (and preferably

Latin) names, to ever smaller variations. In this way some of our native ferns yielded huge numbers of varieties such as Polystichum setiferum, the Soft Shield Fern, which gave over four hundred, and most of all the Lady Fern, Athyrium filix-femina, with over seven hundred.

Yet among all this plethora of plants, inevitably many were first class garden forms. Fortunately, when once the craze was over, the best forms were the ones that tended to survive most successfully in gardens, in the hands of the few remaining enthusiasts, until slowly over time all was forgotten and forgiven. So that today some of the finest garden varieties, especially of our native ferns, still date from the Victorian era. In particular it seems to be the wild finds of the Victorians that are the most exciting: such as Athirium filix-femina, 'Frizelliae', with its charming nickname The Tatting Fern, so-called because the reduced bobble-like foliage of this accommodating dwarf form resembles the threadwork that was used for trimming handkerchiefs and cushions; though it's more correctly referred to as 'Frizelliae' for the Mrs Frizell who accidentally found the plant growing wild in Ireland. Or the plant which takes its name from the reigning monarch herself, Athyrium filix-femina 'Victoriae', found by a student named James Cosh who stepped on the plant while jumping over a wall, and gave the original to be planted at Buchanan Castle in Stirlingshire. It gets its name because the leaves or 'pinna' which break from the main stem in pairs at an angle to each other, form a 'V' – for Victoria of course. It's a truly striking fern because as the leaves leave the stem at an angle, they cross over each other to form a diagonal lattice effect. Additionally, 'Victoriae' is a tall, strong growing and upright plant with a crested edge to the frond, and altogether a real sense of style, which makes it eminently garden worthy.

Lastly it's necessary to bring things up to date, and most of all to look for new beginnings. In recent years many exciting things have begun to happen with ferns and a revival of interest is really underway. Many exciting new foreign species which wouldn't have been available to any but the wealthiest of Victorians have started to appear in our nurseries and garden centres, bringing with them all sorts of thrilling new features such as coloured fronds, and tree ferns at almost affordable prices which were just not available before. Not only that but the new interest in the design aspects of gardens has helped to bring ferns to the fore, as many of them are truly designer plants of the first water. Hopefully we now have enough respect for nature not to go out digging up our wild flora just to fill our gardens, especially as it's now so easy to get what we need from the nursery trade, and raising them from spores is now made relatively simple by modern technology. Let's hope this time in our much more eclectic age ferns will not become objects of obsession but will take their place in gardens for the genuine use, interest, beauty and pure romance that they truly have.

Dead Heading

In the village, there's a small but neat garden belonging to and maintained by a mature couple called John and Mary - gardened by them both, or so I thought for many years. Recently, however, when I walked through the village taking the lane past their front garden, John was working alone in the front garden, Mary having gone in to make tea. So I stopped by the hedge to pass the time of day and compliment John on the results of his efforts, a beautiful mixed cottage garden with both flowers and vegetables; not at all a designer garden but a true traditional and unsophisticated vernacular country garden, of which a few still survive even now, in this old out-of-the-way county.

He wasn't, however, too happy. "I don't know." he said, "It's her garden really, she's just got me doing all this dead-heading stuff. It seems like a waste of time to me, it's really tedious and I'm sure it don't do any good. Can I ask you, does it really work? To my mind most garden jobs are just a complete and boring waste of time. I can't see what people see in it".

Well, strange as it may seem, in some ways I agree with John. Maybe what he says is right, and that for him gardening really is a lost cause which, if it were anyone else might be sad, but I know that if you have a rich and full life like John, who is both a woodsman and a gamekeeper among other things, then you can afford at least a few blind spots. But if you too are beginning to think about following John in his negative views, then let me say just a little about dead heading in particular.

The short answer is, yes John, dead heading doesn't work. At least not all of the time and on all flowers. You do it, of course, in order to stop the plants completing their natural cycles of flowering and then setting seed and, especially if they're perennials, going dormant for the winter. You are, of course, hoping that by removing the flowers soon after they've finished, then the plants, being frustrated, will produce a further crop, and you do it because presumably you prefer flowers to seeds, though this is for some people a questionable taste.

Some flowers on which dead heading won't work are obvious, such as spring bulbs which only flower once a year whatever you do. (Though in fact you may deadhead these in the hope of making a bigger, stronger bulb and larger flower for next year.) And though it works well for many summer flowers, it won't work for all, nor as you may guess will it generally work for late autumn flowers. It also varies a lot with the seasons and with geography – short summers or early frosts may frustrate your efforts, while long mild Indian summers may make it possible to do it even more often, or to greater effect.

Disbudding, which is almost the same thing but you do it before the flowers open, is just as variable. I once disbudded some Cosmos plants which were small and late-planted, in order to make them grow larger. This they did, eventually becoming huge in size but they only opened their first flowers just in time for the frosts, which were early that year, to kill them. It seemed a loss at the time but at least I learned something from it, a something I could never have learned from anyone but my foolish self.

So, how then do you know which plants to dead head and which not to? Sometimes books will give you a clue but that's rare, and they can tell you nothing about each individual season, nor your own local climate. No, the only real way to learn is to try it and see for yourself – just as Mary did, for I'm sure that being a villager of the old type, she never read a gardening book in her life. "After all," Mary would say, "why waste your time reading about things like that when if you're in doubt, you can always ask the neighbours or try it yourself and see".

And it's this John, which makes gardening so exiting, the fact that it's one continuous experiment, with no limit to what you may learn or how many times you may take the gamble, each task a personal science experiment whose outcome can never be precisely predicted. This was the spirit in which I knew Mary gardened, always willing to try something new and regarding a failure as a chance to try again, while repeated failures were simply a little addition to her personal store of gardening wisdom, all to be gained from the adventure. Though I do have some sympathy with you John, because you only get to do the snipping never the planning, or take the final account.

**

It seems sadly that there are a lot of people however, who have an almost phobic aversion to any form of uncertainty. I remember many years ago attending a meeting of a large and highly thought of gardening club. The speaker's subject was a number of quite new plants that were now being introduced, and he was offering a large number of these for sale at the meeting or even free to good homes. Amazingly some of the members present seemed reluctant even to try the free plants, and when I inquired of one why he was reluctant, I was rocked back on my heels by the astounding and belligerent reply. He was, he said, not willing to try a plant if it didn't come with what he called 'proper' cultural information. If the speaker wanted people to grow these plants why did he not write a book and tell them how they should be grown? He came, he said, to these meetings to learn how things should be grown, not be fobbed off by so called 'experts' who said they didn't know anything about the plants as yet.

This seemed to take caution to the extreme. Surely, I thought, coming to a gardening society meeting meant an eagerness to be near the cutting edge, and here was a chance to be exactly that and it was rejected. If the member really wanted to see how to grow these plants put down in print, then surely one of the best ways was to try growing them for himself, and if he succeeded, write it up for the society's journal, and if it failed then what was lost but a few minutes' time and a tiny amount of garden space? It's true that in the professional world where many people spend their working days, there is a premium set upon certainty, often a heavy financial one. This was certainly true of John, for example, in his profession of gamekeeper, where even the slightest doubt about the health of his stock could well entail a real cost, and uncertainty was a luxury only the wealthy and privileged could afford. So perhaps he is the one person we shouldn't judge too harshly in this matter.

But most of us who garden are all, to some degree, amateurs, in the old true sense of the word 'amateur' meaning doing something for the 'love of it'. Think back to the days when rare new plants arrived only after having crossed the oceans in sailing ships, and then only infrequently and at great expense – often in human life as well as money. When the plants had then to be trusted reverently to head gardeners who staked their careers on growing them. Those days are long since gone. Most plants today are relatively cheap in every sense, made so after a very long time by that very process.

Which is why it makes me angry when people are precious about plants and timid in using them. It's a long time since any gardener, even a paid one, was called to the 'big house', cap in hand, to explain why some green thing that cost twice his annual wage could not survive in a stinking London smog. Yes, of course it's a shame if a plant dies, and the hopes we had for it die with it, but the garden space is soon refilled, and perhaps next time with something better, at least with something that better suits that corner. That method is nature's way after all.

The British hedgerow is filled with all the wonderful glories of summer, the tall cow parsley and the delicious dog rose, but those plants only grow at the cost of the ten thousand seeds whose opportunities for growing those few lucky plants stole away, murdering them with smothering shade and toxic root secretions even before their birth. Your garden, too, stands where the wild grasses and the cowslip would otherwise grow. When we garden we choose what we grow and in so doing, we do, by the very nature of how life itself works, also choose what should not grow. Every garden is from the beginning an act of 'gardening genocide' and so by what right do you regard the death of your darling plant as a greater tragedy than the lives of the weeds that you blithely slay in thousands with your hoe? Yet all those wild flowers have died for nothing if you have no adventure in your soul and your gardening, and try to plant nothing more interesting than what you know to be safe, since how then do you learn or grow.

A Bit Of Drawing Work

It is almost always a delight to be commissioned to design or to re-design a garden for someone, though I'm not sure which of the two brings the greatest satisfaction. Conventionally a designer is supposed to be delighted if offered the open option of a blank canvas on which to work out ideas to your own taste. But the garden designer never really has that kind of freedom, because as well as soil, shade, climate and locality, which bring with them a range of exciting challenges, there's always the need to consider the customer who will have to live with (and in) the outcome. And it would be a hard-hearted gardener who left the customer with a garden that was no more than a shallow monument to one's own ego! But if you have any care, you wouldn't really want to anyway, because the customer is as much a part of your inspiration as are the herbs and trees.

Maybe studio based artists feel that the constant requirement to please the buyers is a restriction on their creativity but with a garden the customers are themselves very much a part of the finished work, being involved from the beginning in the creative process. Garden design is very much a social art, and the garden's and your relationship with the customer, learning to understand the customer's needs, are the most important and perhaps the most stimulating parts of the work.

Consequently this means that you must always have in the back of your mind what it is that customers want from their gardens. This varies hugely and learning to interpret the customer's tastes and needs is all part of the fun. Sometimes you get it wrong, of course. I remember one customer whose casual remarks led me to believe that she was very concerned with colour and its effects in the garden. I therefore spent a great deal of time on the colour scheme and managed to produce a design of great chromatic subtlety. As we walked round the garden one day, the lady didn't seem too interested in the proposed combinations of shades that I was pointing out on the plan. She suddenly said: "I'm not really interested in colour schemes – what I really like is just a glorious jumble of colours". Fortunately in that case it was soon put right.

**

There are, however, a number of interesting factors that most people seem to have in common, and over the years I've acquired a little (though far from complete) understanding of some of them. Undoubtedly the most important thing the majority want from their garden is that it should be a place of refuge and peace. Somewhere set apart from their day-to-day lives where they may go to broaden their mental horizons, restore their mind to strength, and refresh their faith in the world. This is the ideal to be aimed for and is fairly easy to understand, but many people seem to be confused about how to accomplish it. The assumption seems to be that a garden needs to be restful – which is fair enough – but unfortunately the idea of restful seems to many people to equate with dull, boring and unambitious.

This leads to the conclusion that an un-dramatic, unimaginative, ordinary and conventionalised garden is not only more than sufficient but exactly what is required to achieve the perfect state of restfulness. I'm quite convinced, however, that this is wrong and needs to be rethought.

To begin with, we need to ask just exactly what it is that we need the garden to do for us in order that we can move to a better state of mind. Surely it is that the garden should grab hold of our minds and send us, as Andrew Marvell put it, 'off to far other worlds'. And it must be by doing this that helps us to forget our worries and routines. Yes of course, we all know we can easily lose ourselves in the garden when we're working in it, but a garden should be about more than work, however much fun the work may be. Which is why I would always hold it important that a garden should not be in any way dull but should contain as much drama as it possibly can. After all, doesn't the very word 'drama' refer to what takes place in a theatre, another place we go to in order to lose ourselves and unleash our minds? Would we be happy with a play that was boring? How then is a garden going to unleash our higher mind and set the lower one at rest, if it doesn't provide some stimulation to the former?

Let me put a practical example to you. Do you have a bird table in your garden, or have you ever sat in a garden and watched the birds? It is, I think, if you are a person with the least sensitivity, rare that you will find any pastime quite so pleasantly distracting and relaxing as watching garden birds going about their daily round. And yet, are the birds still? Do the birds' actions have no drama? Do the sparrows in your garden never squabble? Of course they do! It is precisely the sagas of these 'mini dramas' which makes them so diverting.

Why then do people choose to have a dull garden with dull planting, flat geometric layouts, and nothing which surprises? Yet it's so easy to do something much better. It needn't take long and it certainly needn't be expensive.

**

One thing that seems never to be considered is the third dimension. Far too many gardens are planned with no thought to height and depth, being just flat layouts on the ground, as though they were no more than two dimensional paper plans brought to life. But even a simple change of level, however slight, more than doubles the excitement to be found in any garden. To move soil certainly involves work and thought; if you use the 'cut and fill method', taking the waste from one area to raise another so that every shovel-full moved counts as two, even this takes little time. However, this is a way of making exciting changes which bring great rewards for very little effort. You can, for example, make sunken gardens and raised beds with little strain of the imagination. Even more interesting are sunken paths which, if the cut and fill method is used, can be naturally partnered by raised beds, bringing the double benefit of raising your planting and making the plants seem twice the size.
I once created a dry ditch across a customer's garden; it never held any water but ran right across the garden, starting and ending with a dummy culvert, and crossed in the middle by a bridge. This idea worked so well, and proved so popular that I received orders for two more. I then had to say, "stop and no more" because I feared that I might become stale if I kept doing the same thing over and over.
In Victorian times sunken paths were so widely used that some of the conventional designs had special names, such as 'dolines' which curve and widen like tadpoles. We seem to have lost all this sense of fun for fun's sake in gardening. The modern garden, it seems, has to be no more than a perfect and unchallenging frame for the house, lest presumably, it should commit the ultimate sin of 'affecting the value', though a well planned and interesting garden can surely only enhance it. What this attitude really reflects is an age of growing timidity.

And even if you don't like moving earth, you can add height in a completely different way, with pergolas and other structures, especially in small gardens where trees may give problems. Yet how often do you see a truly brave structure of good proportions that is able to make a statement? But this isn't intended as a practical article on how to garden, the business of extending into the third dimension is only here intended as an example of attitudes to gardening, so let's leave it now and move on.
My dry ditch was, of course, an illusion though a convincing and a sufficiently subtle one (I hope!). I suspect that if there is any good reason why many people become afraid to attempt to inject drama into their gardens, it is because they see that the minority who do so have an unfortunate tendency to resort to illusion – and often bad and unconvincing illusion at that.

**

For some reason garden literature seems to be obsessed with the business of creating illusions. Books on garden design especially, are filled with ready-made formulas for making your garden seem shorter, longer, wider, larger and even smaller, or for hiding the boundaries or making them more visible. Yet it is rare that they ever devote any time to explaining why you should want to do any of these things in the first place. Save in perhaps the cliché case of the very long narrow town garden, for which maybe I admit a case could possibly be made. But most of all why, I wonder, do they not mention the possibility of making your garden more interesting?
Illusions are things that are best avoided in gardens unless you can make them very convincing. You wouldn't expect a stage illusionist to leave the vanished playing card showing from the end of his sleeve. Why therefore do so many garden ponds – especially the ones which pretend to be natural ponds – show three inches of plastic liner round the edges? Even worse, why do people who build water features, make such elemental mistakes, as perching them half way up dry grassy slopes, retaining them in place with mean narrow rock work dams that could never be watertight in nature? If you are creating an illusion, surely it's important to make it even more real than reality?
If for example someone really wished to suggest the presence of water on a dry grassy slope, why not simply excavate a hollow that meanders down the slope and plant this with plants which look like waterside plants? In this way it would just suggest that water might

sometimes flow down the slope, and leave it at that. That would be so much more a subtle hint or sketch of an illusion that it would be hard to find fault with, yet it would be no less dramatic or interesting. Of course some gardens are complete illusions from beginning to end – the landscape style of the eighteenth century for example, or most oriental gardens with their stylised natural landscapes, and even miniature plants and gardens. But in these cases the area is almost always enclosed and is at least true to itself as a whole, or else a great deal of time and trouble has been used to make the illusion almost perfect.

One other set of oriental ideas that have, however, recently become fashionable, are those that are loosely, and (dare I say it?) quite inaccurately, lumped under the term 'feng-shui'. It is considered that one of the most important aspects of the feng-shui garden is its entrance, providing, it is said, not only physical but also spiritual and mental separation from the outside world, and is therefore most important in helping the garden visitor achieve the correct frame of mind before they have fully entered the garden.

The entrance is often made deliberately narrow, twisted through sharp angles, given high thresholds or, to western eyes, made very large and grand relative to the often tiny gardens they hide. All these entrances, however, have one thing in common, which is that they are all intended to gain the visitor's notice, and slow them down. They say to the visitor that, 'this space is special, not to be dismissed lightly, please take your time to notice'. And although I think that this is a lesson that all gardeners should learn, yet the truth is that this whole idea is not a new import from the east at all – you can find exactly the same ideas about gardens, and especially their entrances, in many of the best western gardens and a lot of our gardening literature, going back for at least two centuries.

**

One of the happiest customers I ever had, asked me to create a garden in an old orchard. This lay at the bottom of the back garden, on the other side of a high hedge, and a damp hollow which may once have been a drain. In order to open the new garden up, we made a hole in the hedge, which we made into an arched gateway. Then we put in a bridge over the hollow which we deepened to make a true water feature. I think that one reason why this customer was so happy in the end with the finished garden was that to reach it, you had first to cross the old garden, then pass through the arch and finally over the bridge, by which time it must have been hard to avoid the feeling that you had been on a journey and had entered a new world of pleasures.

Though I don't think that we in Britain will ever need to go quite so far as some oriental gardeners who sometimes even put extra false gates within the garden to mark the transitions within; it always surprises me that here in Britain especially, where we have such a long tradition of gardening, we don't seem to spend much time or effort on the entrances to our gardens. This is such an easy way to give some feeling of worth to our garden spaces, and if we can manage that, then we will make them, and the time we spend in them, seem all that more special.

And so, of all the things that are guaranteed to please the garden owner in the long term I think that these two, namely, a sense of entrance, and the quality of using all three dimensions, are perhaps the most important.

Crab Apple

The new crab apple tree (Malus 'Red Sentinel') is already an important feature in my garden, partly because my garden is small enough for even quite a little tree to have a starring role, but also because it has two really great performances in its repertoire. The first comes in the spring when it is thickly covered in multi-coloured blossom, and the second through the autumn and winter when it hangs heavy with bright red fruit. At which time, like the best old performer, it spins out this last act out for all it's worth, often in recent mild winters keeping a good display of fruit until March.
The frost resilience of the fruit is truly amazing, and the winter-hardy apples look spectacular hanging nearly as thick as grapes on the bare branches, and especially beautiful with a cap of white snow on each miniature crab, the bright red and glistening white reflecting perfectly the traditional Yuletide colourings. Perhaps because it brings the brightest colour scheme it can to the garden in the very darkest days of all. I've never attempted to pick the fruit or make anything from it, though you easily could, for even an ornamental crab like this should be just as edible as any other, but we have no shortage of fruits for jam-making and it's a pleasant luxury just to enjoy the show for its own sake.

**

The winter of 2009/2010 was a lot harder than any that my 'teenage' crab has ever seen before, and the fruit didn't last beyond mid-December, even though it didn't seem to suffer at all from the frost. As soon as the snow became reasonably deep and hard, a large flock of fieldfares and a couple of redwings appeared and stripped away all the fruit in a quick couple of days. Their arrival took me by surprise and all I was aware of was a great clatter of wings retreating in haste when I went on my usual morning tour of the garden.
However, the following day I crept down more carefully and was able to watch the hectic feasting and squabbling, but even when hungry, they're still shy birds and it's hard to get close. Even if I hadn't seen it with my own eyes, it wouldn't have been hard to tell what

happened because the snow beneath the tree, and for some four or five feet around it was stained, not red but bright candy floss pink. Though it was hard to know just how this was achieved since, save for five or six places where scuffles in the snow had exposed the soil underneath, the staining was very even, and there was little sign of any excrement, nor was there much evidence of any major spillage, since except for a few odd bits of apple skin they seem to have been very tidy eaters. I can only assume that a very little crab apple juice dripped from a hungry beak must go a long way and stain an awful lot of snow!

This particular crab never had this sort of attention from the birds before, and it was interesting to see that a couple of the local blackbirds and at least one thrush joined in the feast and disputed aggressively for them; though they hadn't touched the crabs before the fieldfares arrived. It made me wonder, therefore, were they simply responding to the same conditions of season and climate as the fieldfares and therefore began to feed on the same source at exactly the same time, or were they attracted to the crabs by the fieldfares' activities? It's widely thought that birds tend to find most of their food by watching other birds, but does this only apply just to the individual source of food, or to the generic type of nutrition as well? It will be interesting to see what happens next year now that a possible future habit has been started. Will the garden birds remember what happened this year and start on the crabs without prompting from the fieldfares, or will they wait for hard weather and the arrival of the Scandinavian migrants to show them the way again? Perhaps it's a universal truth which applies to all animals (and not just humans) that we need foreigners to teach us the value of our own parishes. It will be a good test of this if it's a mild winter again next season.

I didn't, of course, have the usual fruit to enjoy the following spring but what does that matter since I had a lot of fun watching the birds, and had the satisfaction of getting closer to the normally wild and shy fieldfares than I have in a long time.

I know some gardeners including one in my own village who get terribly worked up about this sort of thing, and would even talk about digging up the tree because of the lost fruit, though you can only loose fruit if you have it in the first place. I don't know why I do so, but I think that they must be the same people who write letters to the newspapers protesting, (And I don't know who they think they are protesting to), about the birds of prey who 'steal' the songbirds from their gardens and bird tables, as though the summer is responsible for stealing spring from the calendar.

PS Since that year the birds have never returned, and my snow now is always white.

Customers And Other Tender Things

I often struggle with plants that many growers in England, Wales and Western Scotland find quite hardy, especially some of the foreign species. So a few winters ago when the BBC declared us to be the most cut off village in England, and they sent reporters in a (naturally vain) attempt get here. They got to within ten miles, and found a person to interview who vaguely knew someone who lives here... Well, that winter provided a really first class hardiness test for a number of the foreign species.

So that it was also pleasant to see the return of many exotic species of plants – both perennials and shrubs as well as my ferns – the following spring. What's really surprising about this, however, is how hard it can be to market them, despite the fact that many are bold, strong-growing, hardy, adaptable and attractive, which should surely be more than enough to sell them to the most careful of buyers. Not to mention that they often have the seeming advantage of being a little bit different from the average plant.

The resistance to buying many exotic plants on the part of the gardening public, however, still continues to mystify me. Gardening literature is full of demands for nurseries to provide a greater diversity of plants; most gardeners profess to be in search of something that differs a little from the norm, and many customers will tell me that they're visiting my nursery precisely because they want to find something a bit unusual. Yet these same people eventually leave quite happily carrying a basket filled with a good sample of all the most usual suspects. And this even when the less ordinary ferns have been pointed out to them as much better suited to their needs, and often at their own request. I know it's almost certainly the case that to many gardeners, ferns generally may still count as something frighteningly different from common garden plants but can it really be the case that there are degrees of 'different', and if there are, what is the downside to 'different' when you're buying plants for your garden?

It's true that there is a growing trend, which started five or six years ago – perhaps on the back of the popular wildflower meadow fashion – to value even more the British native plants in the garden, and in many ways I think that's a wonderful thing. But even when they're only buying collections of exotics, many gardeners still show a sad lack of adventure. Unfamiliar and hard-to-remember names may have a lot to do with it, and that may be forgiven; though I

would rather have a beautiful plant with a forgotten name, than a boring one that I can remember.
Worst of all however, worries about hardiness are often sited as the reason, and of course hardiness is a real and important issue. Yet sometimes I think that the way in which hardiness is so often treated as an absolute (in gardening literature especially) has a lot to answer for. Classing plants as either hardy or not, according to lines drawn on a climate map, which seems to be the best stab at the problem most books make is, to my mind, not very helpful. Much better and more honest would be to talk about risk levels rather than absolutes, based maybe on numbers of years.

**

For example the beautiful little Mountain Avens, Dryas oxipetala, is perhaps about the hardiest plant you could name. A low creeping plant, it has soft grey felted leaves and bright yellow, often orange streaked, flowers similar to small roses in shape. It isn't difficult to place in the garden, as long as it's not in damp shade, and is well worth its space as an easy alpine. In the wild, however, it grows today only high in the hills of the north and is quite rare. Yet once it was one of the few plants to grow widely in the British Isles, in the cold frosty time at the end of the Ice Age, it being, like the dwarf willows and birches, a typical plant of the Arctic tundra. Indeed so common is its pollen in fossil peat deposits that it gives its name to a couple of the slightly warmer spells which interrupted the ice ages, namely the younger and elder 'Dryas'.
Yet even the Mountain Avens didn't grow in Britain at the height of the ice ages when the glaciers completely covered the land, only returning at last some twelve thousand years ago as the ice retreated. So in a sense you could say that although it is perhaps the hardiest plant you're likely to grow in your garden, it's not really truly hardy every year. It is, in fact, only approximately hardy in some twelve thousand out of twelve thousand and one years, so we can therefore conclude that no plant, not even Dryas, can ever really be considered completely hardy.
At the other end of the scale is the common Pelagonium which practically no gardener would say is a hardy plant. After all, even well-known chains of garden centres (which are not noted for being sceptical on matters of hardiness) sell them only as 'summer bedding' plants. Yet for many years I knew of a Lincolnshire garden,

admittedly on the coastal side of the Wolds, where Pelagoniums were often left out in the winter, and in at least two winters out of the twenty or so that I knew them, they came through in good health. You could therefore call them 'one year in ten' hardy plants.
In between come things such as some of the larger leaved Penstemons and many Euphorbias which were always traditionally regarded as not hardy in the north but which gained great popularity a few years ago following a couple of decades' worth of mild winters. Then along came the winter of 2010 and suddenly they're re-classified by many people as tender once more. Yet really would it not be much better to say that they're not really tender but only hardy plants in nineteen years out of twenty? And if I was a gambling person, then would I not consider that for the pleasure of having such beauties in my garden, then, nineteen to one on, was a fairly good bet.
And plants are cheap. Yes they are! You can buy five or ten that will last at least a year or two, or indeed many, for the price of a reasonable meal out, which will only last an hour or two.
Is this not really a much better way to look at things, to accept a roughly defined degree of risk, regarding plants as hardy in a given percentage of years, perhaps? Rather than try to force nature, which tends to suffer from the annoying quality of being practically seamless anyway, into climate zones drawn by humans on a paper map. Perhaps it's better to think of plants in terms of so many years' hardy. After all we all accept the principle of half-hardy annuals and bedding plants for one year only so why not think of two, three or five-season hardy plants as worth planting. I often plant, for example, the wonderful insect flower Verbena Bonarensis and hope for more than one season out of it.
I know that the problem is really with we humans; we do tend to like things neat and fitted into simple easy-to-understand, unambiguous categories: hardy, and not hardy, or moisture-loving, and dry soil et cetera. Yet doesn't this take away the whole adventure of gardening, which should be about discovery, and discoveries are surely made only by taking risks. Take the case of my Artemisia, for example, which I planted in the garden many years ago. Its likes are dry soil and sun, so that was where I planted it and being happy it throve. In fact, although very beautiful, it grew so well it proved to be quite a nasty thug, growing rapidly through all its neighbours and strangling many of them before I could even get to it with a fork.
So I dug it up intending to get rid of it but, noticing once more that it

was very beautiful, I spared it and dropped a small part in a temporary hole, intending to move it again. However, naturally being a gardener with other things to do, I never got round to it, and despite the fact that the new place was in a shady wet hollow, it continued to thrive and remained beautiful. With the one difference that though still growing well, it had now lost all its thuggish invasive habits. Perhaps it is now just a little less happy, or maybe it took its punishment as a sign and realised that the compost heap awaits those who annoy the gardener too much!

There's a lot to be gained by ignoring the gardening books, and for examples, let me give you a short list: Osmunda regalis, Athyrium filix-femina, Onoclea sensibilis and Matteuccia. You don't need to know the plants, only that they're all listed in most, if not all, the textbooks I've read, as requiring a lime-free, acid, humus-rich soil. My garden is on the top of the chalk Wolds, thin and dry with lumps of the alkaline white stuff showing through. (And go on, for the sake of space, I will leave you to guess the next bit.) Yet had I only listened to the textbooks, would I have them now? I think you know the answer...

Watering

Autumn always seems to come much faster than I think and catches me out. Human perceptions seem to be, in so many subtle ways, self-adjusting mechanisms that automatically recalibrate themselves without our being aware of it, so that we never realise how dim a well-lit room is until we step out into the daylight, or how bright the snowy day, until we go inside. But we seem to be especially poor at perceiving most of the bigger changes in the environment, particularly if they take place over anything more than an hour or two.

We all know that sooner or later there comes a day in autumn when the temperature first drops below five degrees Celsius, we'll shiver dramatically and jokingly tell each other how cold it is. Yet without our being aware of it, during the course of the winter our bodies adjust and our perceptions change completely, so that in spring when the first day hits five once again, we comment on the mildness; we can't wait to take our heavy clothes off and to walk about in shirt sleeves. It's only when we encounter things outside of our own skins that we are suddenly forced to adjust our thinking to the real changes.

**

It's mainly for this reason that the change in the nursery from the summer watering to the winter irrigation regime always seems to catch me off guard, surprising me with its apparent suddenness. In early August we're already nearly two months from the longest day, and yet the plants are drinking heavily as if it were high summer still, needing to be well watered each day at least, and often sometimes even this seems not to be enough. Yet just a couple of weeks later the needs of the plants seem to be well satisfied with just one good watering every other day, and even with this they're often getting a little over wet.

I turn a plant out of its pot, holding its rootball in my hands and think to myself that this is damp enough, and I'll soon be over-watering, so that I'll find a truly soggy smelling mess if I'm not careful. Then again a couple of weeks later, as soon as mid September comes round, watering once every three days seems to be all that's needed; and it requires just a week or two of this before six or seven days can be missed out without any problem. By which time even my insensitive human senses start to feel the decline of the year, and I know that only two or three more waterings will take us through to the deep winter when the nursery will hardly need irrigation at all, not even the coddled plants under glass. Yet the change nearly always catches me out, and I hardly ever respond to it quite quickly enough.

It doesn't take much thought to realise the reason why this should be so. We know for example, that the day length changes much more rapidly near the equinoxes of autumn and spring, than it does in midsummer and winter. The summer and winter solstices – whose names mean 'the standing still of the sun' – get their names from the fact that in ancient times without the benefit of modern instruments, people could not discover any significant change in day length for at least a few days around mid-summer and mid-winter. For the changes in the relative length of day and night must take time to get going, especially towards and away from summer and winter solstices, till they race though spring and autumn, fastest at the equinox, and then slowing once more gradually back down as they near each solstice, so that the big seasons of winter and summer really do 'linger', as we say.

But there's much more to it than that. Partly I think that our poor perception of the changing days is that most of us tend to think only of one end of the day. In the autumn we're either early risers and think to ourselves that the mornings are getting darker, or we're night owls and think that it grows dark soon these days. Few of us poor introverted humans really notice, in a fully aware way, that we are losing the day at both ends.

Nor, though we may know it intellectually, are we often really aware of how much lower in the sky, and therefore less powerful, the sun is becoming. The tragedy of winter is that not only do we get a much shorter day, but that what we effectively lose is the hot burning centre of the day, the high summer noon when the sun is at its most powerful, leaving us only the equivalent of the pallid early morning and faded late evening, joined together in the middle. The sun's power is therefore being nibbled away in three ways, shortened from both ends and turned down in magnitude.

When you then add to this the fact that many plants are actively beginning to prepare for winter, slowing down their metabolism, as nature programmes them to do, it is then a transparent wonder that their need for water crashes so rapidly in autumn. And also that the plants, though they have no eyes, may yet perceive the whole of the sun far better than we do, precisely because they lack our hot blood, which makes our own small inner environment more important to us than the large outer.

Plants, on the other hand, can only stand literally rooted to the spot, living at the ambient temperature and responding totally to the magnitude of all that happens around them. They perceive the seasons' changes by standing and absorbing them for days and nights on end in ways we introspective and self-absorbed humans, for whom an hour is too long to concentrate, cannot even begin to imagine. Once more, whether I like it or not, I am outwitted by a plant.

Catkins And Seasons

Those who garden also love to play games and gossip, and the annual cycles are nearly always at the heart of the fun. The gardener always has an eye for the year's changes and notes carefully the first arrival of each new season's flowers, discussions of which form the backbone of endless small talk. Yet it seems to me that if you listen carefully you will always hear the same cast of characters – hellebores and snowdrops in winter, roses in summer, asters in autumn and, most of all, crocuses and daffodils in spring. Yet this makes for a very short and unimaginative list, wouldn't you agree?

Missing from this list, and what you hardly ever hear of, even in the anxious and impatient days of spring, is the opening of catkins on plants such as the willow and hazel. Though we were all charmed by them when we were young – if only because to children these 'flowers without petals' seem so strange and different – gardeners often seem to be just as unaware of the great number, and the ecological importance of these wind pollinated flowers, as is everyone else. But let me challenge you to go back and look at them again with your adult's more discerning eye, and then deny to me their beauty.

In many ways a good argument could be made for catkins as a far better marker of spring's progress than the flowering bulbs, for however late in opening they may be, the bulbs are still really flowers of the winter. This is not only because they grow from food stores laid down the previous summer and kept as winter reserves but their whole life strategy is that by storing food, they may steal the march on all the other plants and get most of their vital work done before the larger woody plants start to cast their shade.

Even the bulb's method of growing is a clever adaptation to the cold of winter, since in early spring the temperature is often too cold for plant cells to divide and multiply efficiently, building up new tissues in the normal way by real growth, as most woody plants do. For bulbs that is near impossible. What they do instead is to grow by expanding their existing cells, making them larger by inflating them with water and salts, like someone using a hydraulic jack or filling balloons from a tap. This is of course a subtle and wonderful adaptation on the bulb's part, and the main secret of their success, helping them to get some of their work done before the competition even wakes up. But it is to my mind yet another good, if entirely human and subjective reason, for regarding spring bulbs as the last of the winter flowers. That may seem eccentric but since the seasons blend continuously into one another and the divisions between them are entirely human and subjective anyway, I would claim that we are each of us entitled to put the divisions where we wish.

The catkins of willow, alder and hazel, however, are truly a sign of the coming spring if only because they're found on woody plants whose leafing and seeding life stretches right through the summer. Yet even these cleverly take advantage of the leafless spring to shed their wind-carried pollen into the free and open air before the summer leaves can close the gale-swept spaces between the boughs.

Moreover, though we don't think of them as such, catkins are in every way true flowers, and not just simple clumps of hairs as some people imagine but elaborate structures with multiple layers of hairs and scales, often with their pollenia on stalks and the remains of their protective scales at their base. And there is far more variety than you might think. In fact, the wind pollinated flowers are as varied in form and method of working as the familiar insect pollinated blooms. If you doubt this, forget just for a minute the well-known catkins of willow, alder and hazel, and look closely at some of the less familiar flowers of trees, such as ash and oak. You will then find a range of wind pollinated structures that vary as much as roses from orchids.

**

One New Year's day, it being one of the coldest winters for several years, with the ground frozen iron hard and snow sitting unthawed after nearly a month, I happened to pass some hazel bushes while walking the dog. I felt the catkins and found them hard enough to bend a fingernail. In the depth of winter, the male catkins of the hazel take the form of small sausage-shaped dangling buds, and in the coldest weather they feel hard to the touch, almost as if they were made of wood. If you look closely at this stage, you'll see that the scales forming on the outside of the catkins are arranged in perfect spirals winding down the length.

I decided to see how quickly they would respond if given some warmth and shelter. So I broke off a couple of twigs and put them in a vase of water on my bedroom windowsill fairly close to the warmth of a radiator. Within five days the catkins had enlarged and started to soften considerably, and a couple of days later two out of the four had started to shed pollen. We can conclude then, that opening and shedding are at least susceptible to, if not mainly controlled by, temperature rather than day length, as you might expect in spring; and by February of that year, following just a short mild spell, the hazels had come out in the hedgerow, despite the earlier cold winter.

At the same time the dark sombre-foliaged yew trees at the bottom of my garden, especially the males, also showed their flowers, (not strictly catkins as yew is a conifer). Yew flowers are like little golden balls half-hidden among the leaves. Few flowers, even the insect pollinated, could be quite so bright in colour as these dazzling little pearls of gold which shed clouds of gold dust if tapped. Enough gold, in fact, to excite a prospector, that is if they were merely dead mineral particles and not complex living things, packed full of coded information and living potential sufficient to grow a tree, help it find all it needs, and fight off its enemies for a period of a thousand years or more.

Which raises a question that I suspect I will never be able to answer. It might seem obvious to suppose that the wind pollinated flowers are less noticeable because they have no need to attract insects and other pollinators, yet many of them are far from being shy or dull, often showing bright colours, not only in the pollen itself but also in the bracts which cover and surround them. The so-called 'pussy willows' make a brave show of gold and cream in spring, more than bright enough to rival any flowering bulbs, even showy narcissus. So is this just an accident or is it intended, and if it is intended, to what purpose and to whom is the display directed? Obviously no plant would want to advertise vital organs in which it had invested a lot of resources, as well as its hopes for the future, if that meant making them more vulnerable to things that could eat them.

This means then that there are at least three possible reasons for the colours. The first is that the colours are unavoidable, come accidentally and are no great disadvantage to the plant, especially those that flower early before many animals are active, though I feel that this reason is very unlikely, and just blowing in the wind for the sake of it. The second is that the colours are defensive, intended to make the flowers look like sick, malnourished or poisonous shoots which no animal would want to eat. Again, certainly possible, though again I think it unlikely.

Which leaves a third rather intriguing possibility. It's just possible that there are very few totally wind pollinated plants at all. That if for example, a rare early insect should visit one of these catkins to feed on pollen, then there's a real possibility that when it departs, an accidental chance transference of pollen to a female flower may take place, raising the likelihood of a successful pollination, even if it's only a slightly enhanced possibility. Nature would tend to favour anything which helps the process of fertility, and that is, no doubt, how pollination by insects began in the first place. But what is really interesting about this possibility is the fact that not only were wind and insect pollinations not mutually exclusive in the past, but there's no reason why they should be today.

Moreover there's no reason why we should not see a complete spectrum, from plants that rely entirely on wind, like most grasses, all the way through plants which are half-and-half, to the true insect specialists. And in the centre we should not expect to find not just plants that are in a state of balance, or those evolving from wind to animal vectors but – since nature rarely moves in straight lines – we might expect to find a few that are in the process of moving the other way, from animals to wind. Nature is rarely simple or straightforward, nor is it a case of 'wind primitive and insect advanced'. There must be a large number of complex and often interacting factors involved in a plant's ecological economy which would tend to favour one method of pollination or the other. Plants which often grow in large stands could cheaply use the wind, while rare plants in narrow niches need long distance and highly targeted vectors, and no doubt the balance of economy is fine and delicate. I don't know if any research has ever been done on this by botanists but since it would be a very large undertaking I suspect very little, even if the results would make a fascinating read.

**

Alders, usually found along the stream banks and in the wet places, mainly in the less cultivated areas of the country since the alder is a tree for which modern forestry and agriculture has little time, are also early and show classic catkins very like the hazel. Yet it is almost worth making a journey just to see the alder in full flower, especially since it's one of the few trees where the female flowers are quite impressive. Interestingly, they resemble small pinecones, and they remain on the trees long after they have shed their seeds, so that most of the alders usually show a good display of both male catkins and female cones at the same time.

A few of the many different willows also fall into the spring/early summer flowering season, and are perhaps the best known of the wind flowers after the hazel. The earliest are the osiers such as the purple willow, often known collectively as the 'pussy willows'. These are the hedgerow bushes with the small furry tufts of flowers appreciated by everyone as something special. The later flowering willows all have much more loose open catkins, which makes the dense furry tufts of the early osiers almost certainly an adaptation to the cold weather of late winter.

Soon after that comes the spring proper, with the plethora of birches and maples, which often have large colourful flowers to rival the best of animal pollinated flowers; every year without fail, the Acer 'Crimson King' on my driveway is covered with pendulous golden clusters set off by bronze sepals. Almost last of all come the colourful and spectacular oaks and the ashes with their flowers stained dark imperial purple, flowering as we move slowly towards summer, among much more competition from the animal pollinated plants. And by the time we get to them, I think you will agree, the list of what could be called 'disregarded flowers' begins to look like quite a long one.

Then the year moves on again, and the summer begins for most gardeners with the roses, and you would think that there would now be enough insects flying and running about by then to tip the balance completely in favour of the animal pollinated flowers. Yet why should summer not begin with the flowering of the grasses? Another group of wind pollinated plants, and a group which is so large, modern and important, that it forces you to accept that even in high summer, wind pollination is still a realistic alternative method of insemination, despite the abundance of helpful animals and plenty of leafy barriers to interrupt the air flow.

The grasses are certainly more common than roses, more ecologically and economically important, and their flowers probably make a greater visual impact on the environment as a whole than those of the more regarded rose flowers, even when the wild dog roses abound in every hedgerow. But how many people – excepting those who suffer from hay fever – really note when the flowering of the verges begins in the same way that we always seem to remember the first flowering of the hedgerows. Though it only takes a moment's thought to make a seasonal ritual for yourself, one that is both different and original, and no less as profound and joyous. Then the seasons turn once again, and perhaps in autumn we do eventually notice some at least of the wind's effects because the nuts of hazel, and so many of the trees' seeds, such as ash keys and acorns, are as well noted for their arrival and passing as apples and rose hips – if only because we have to work hard raking them off the lawn! (Though we may not notice the shedding of the grasses' seeds so much, vital as this is, even to our human economies.)

Then last in the cycle comes winter with all its dramatics, merging eventually into spring again. And it is in then that I have an unfulfilled and perhaps quirky little project of my own on which to work... The grass stems stand tall and proud even into the winter, long after they've shed their seeds, and along with them are the dry brown stalks of the cow parsley and several other herbaceous plants of the verges and hedgerows. But when late summer comes round again these are all gone, or seemingly so.

Which might give you a clue as to what it is that I so desperately want to find the time to observe thoroughly. What I want to know is, when do they finally give up and collapse? They mostly seem to stay erect even into the early spring, and I've often wondered if the snow has any effect, for though they sometimes seem to come through the snow well, I'm inclined to think that the snowier winters bring them down more quickly. But I've not been able to confirm this with proper close observation, nor do I know much of the differences between species or regions. So many more questions keep pouring into my mind, and the seasons seem so filled in any case.

It could well be argued that people who are lucky enough to live in the temperate regions are the most fortunate people on earth – not just because of the overall benefits that stem from the climate, or the undoubted economic advantages, but if only because they can enjoy the numerous pleasures that come from the richest of all seasonal cycles. Particularly those four great traditional seasons so widely celebrated in all the classical arts.

Would it not truly be a great shame to miss a single season out of any lifetime, or to wish one away, as we sometimes do when waiting for winter to end in anticipation of spring? In the end, there are but four seasons in a year and perhaps sixty chances to make that fundamental connection in most adults' lives – not really all that many opportunities to note their passage, and not to miss even a single one is almost a duty that you owe yourself. I sometimes think that the ultimate luxury in a busy and time-starved world would surely be to spend at least year of your life to do nothing more than observe the seasons in their passing.

Christmas Trees

For some years now, having a little ground to spare around the nursery, father grew a few Christmas trees in a – perhaps misguided – attempt to supplement his pension by earning a little extra pocket money at the more expensive end of the year. The trees he grew were simply the common Norway Spruce which he planted in straight lines about three feet apart, in any odd corner of the land that wasn't wanted for anything else at the time.

The business was very rustic and set up on an extremely low capital outlay, since he already had most of the things needed, a spade, axe and saw, and he could borrow a rotavator to clear the ground. He then scrounged an old cash tin that was found in the potting shed, and persuaded me to paint 'Xmas Trees' on an old board for the end of the drive – in fact the only things he ever bought were the seedling trees themselves.

The enterprise did not, and could never have, made him a fortune, but then it didn't have to, since like many of the ways country people find to syphon off a little town-made wealth, it had cost him so little financially that it hardly mattered.

It did however bring, as these things usually do, many unforeseen costs and benefits. There certainly were some considerable social benefits, since for several weeks before Christmas we benefited from large numbers of extra visitors trooping in through the gate all day long. Apparently it's assumed that a Christmas tree seller isn't supposed to keep office hours. Many of the visitors were strangers, and throughout the time he sold the trees we made a number of new acquaintances. Many, however, were people we already knew, who regarded the trees mainly as an excuse for visiting. Most of these were welcome, since in the country summer visitors are common enough to become a nuisance, but for some inexplicable reason I've never been able to discover, the supply of people wanting to visit you in the country seems to dry up in the winter.

Father also got plenty of exercise from the business during the dark months, though for a man in his late seventies it always seemed questionable, to my mother at least, if it really was all that beneficial to be employed digging holes on wet windy nights in December. Father, however, didn't mind the physical work quite so much as the waiting, because choosing a Christmas tree is a serious business and the whole ritual, apparently, takes quite a lot of time.

**

First of all the whole of the buyer's family must be assembled, down to the smallest child and the most distant cousin, which quite often involves arriving in two or more vehicles, which are then carefully parked for an optimum getaway. All must be disembarked, dressed warmly against the cold and booted up before the first member of the group is permitted to move off. Nor can the choosing begin until the whole group has progressed to the far end of the field and reported in, because when choosing a tree the roles of each family member are strictly prescribed, in what generally today seems an almost quaint, if not positively sexist way.
The smallest children are first sent out as scouts to find appropriate trees, whilst the youngest woman present supervises them, and the older men do the important business of engaging father in small talk. And when the youngest woman has received the reports of the children, then the more mature women in the group will make the final decision which usually involves a strictly observed ritual of overruling the men, who generally only participate in the decision-making process with such unhelpful and easily overruled comments as, "It's too big", "Too small" or, "It won't fit in the car." And finally – what is the man's most important role if not to carry the tree and load it into the car!
There are of course exceptions. Every year sees the arrival of at least one fashionable young woman in a tiny car, who is no doubt furnishing her first new home in the hope of making good impression on friends and relatives, and who invariably comes to walk the winter fields in high heels. "There's mud! What! Between here and the trees?" "Have you nothing else to wear?" asks father, in his best patient mode. "I've got sandals?"

**

Most of the demand is for the smaller domestic-sized trees, and inevitably there's a surplus of trees which have grown too large, though a few of these still find a sale to schools, churches and village halls, and the like. One regular customer is the village wag, because among all the other roles that the large, round, bearded and genial man takes on for the village, is helping to organise the Christmas decoration of the village hall. He is at least he's able to make a quick decision, and usually picks one of the first trees he

comes to, only of course to be overruled by his wife, but he is thicker skinned if not craftier than most men and usually changes the choice back again when he arrives the second time with his small gang of helpers who help to transport and erect the tree.
Whether his wife notices or not, I don't know, but she no doubt cuts him some slack, because no doubt about it, he does get things done. In fact it's hard to know how many of the village's activities would ever get done without him, helping as he does with the village hall's social calendar, the bowling teams and most of all the printing, editing, distributing and most of the writing of the village newsletter. Not all of this is always appreciated of course – it's in the nature of village life that you can never please more than half of the people at any one time, and that anything that does please half of the people is bound to really annoy the other half.
Such a problem occurred when he first started to publish his village newsletter. Unfortunately despite the effort of filling its twenty-odd pages full of articles, letters, advertisements, useful announcements, pictures of the church (plus a few printing errors), he still felt it needed more. So in the interests of lightening up the pages, he added quite a few jokes, and this was where the problems started.

Even more unfortunately, as a former merchant seaman, his idea of what constituted a good joke didn't tally with that of the Women's Institute, who immediately threatened a boycott, if not very nearly an actual public burning of the publication. This naturally only made him all the more determined and he dug his heels in ever more deeply, and starting to insert even more colourful material.
The problem was eventually solved by his wife, who stepped in once more. and undertook to censor the jokes. Fortunately he still manages to slip in a few references on his pet subjects but now it's much more of a challenge for him to get away with it, which may not be too bad because every pensioner needs a bit of a challenge.

**

But I digress. Even when buying the normal sized trees, no two customers are alike, and it's amazing the range of choices that are required for such a simple product as a Christmas tree: cut off, dug up, bare-rooted, delivered, taken now, marked for collection later, wrapped in a bag or supplied with a pot and sand. Father was kept busy for several weeks each winter filling the demand, and the work

went right up to the last hour, because there's always a customer or two who want their plants on Christmas Eve.
But at least there was some gratitude, with many people taking the trouble to tell him how much they enjoyed the trees, and strangely how much they enjoyed the fact that his trees never seemed to drop any needles. This is apparently a problem so common with many Norway Spruce that advice on how to care for a tree and prevent this horrible occurrence is widespread in much of the media. There are even special (though according to rumour not very successful) varieties of tree available which don't drop; while some trees are specially cultivated or given fertilizer to achieve the desired non-dropping quality. I must say though, that father always received many compliments on how well his trees kept their needles, and he never did any of this. He simply sold fresh ones.

Blackbirds And Others

If I were asked to pick a bird that deserved the title of domestic familiar, then I do not think I would choose the classic Robin, for me it would be the blackbird, as no bird is quite so ever-present in the garden or such a constant cause of amusement to any gardener. What could be more familiar than the loud clatter of the blackbird's alarm note rattling away, usually telling us that either we, or a neighbourhood cat, have been spotted, behaving much less discreetly than the blackbird who owns the garden thinks we should do.

One spring a few years ago I was asked to help sort out a neglected garden so that the elderly owner could continue with its maintenance by herself. It only took a few days to clear the borders of weeds, restore the lawn and prune the shrubs but by the time I was finished, that brief period was more than enough for me to have formed a close relationship with one of the local blackbirds. A small brown hen bird with a distinctive white flash on her wing, she would come hopping along at regular intervals, cocking her head on one side in a charming manner to eye the ground around me carefully.

By the end of the week she was an almost constant companion, following me round the garden, picking up the insects and worms that I exposed when digging. I never found out where she was nesting but I suspect it was in a neighbouring garden, because she usually flew off in that direction whenever she was well fed or grew bored with me. She was not visible for a lot of the time, especially if I was doing something like painting or working on the lawnmower, but she must have been nearby and observing me acutely because she always appeared as soon as I switched to a task such as digging, which was likely to produce something to eat.

What interested me was how she was able to do this. Was she was able to reason by observing the nature of my movements that I was likely to be turning up food? Did she visit me regularly and then leave before I noticed her when there was nothing of interest, or did she observe particularly the earth being turned? It's quite possible that she was more than patient and intelligent enough to understand my usefulness, and indeed might well have been helped by some hard-wired instinct associated with large animals rooting in the ground, that she inherited from her ancestors.

Like the familiar robin who, it is believed by some people, is instinctively programmed to follow creatures like buffalo and wild pigs as they turn up the soil, and who therefore found it easy to switch it to humans when we invented spades and ploughs – though it seems, incidentally, that robins only behave like this in Britain. Continental robins are, I'm told, shy woodland creatures which rarely venture into gardens.

But it's also possible that it was just the ground itself that she watched because her powers of observation in many other respects were quite amazing. After only a couple of days she was coming to within less than an arm's length of me, regularly plunging her beak into the ground, then pulling up to swallow worms and other invertebrates. Yet although I was standing so close to her, I hardly ever saw the things that she found until they were already pulled out, and I would guess that for every creature I was able to observe on the newly-turned earth, she was able to see ten at least, often pulling out large juicy worms from places where I had looked closely and would have sworn there were none.

On the last day it was time to dig over the vegetable patch, and as I would soon be leaving, I decided to try an experiment. Sorting out some of the largest and most tempting worms that I could find, and offering them directly to my new friend by hand. But although she was quite happy to hunt quite close to my feet, especially from behind when my back was turned, she would not come onto my hand and became quite wary at anything less than a finger length. I am sure that given time enough I could have trained her to come and feed from my hand, just as you would with a robin, but over-taming a wild animal is perhaps not the best thing to do anyway.

**

The robin is well known for its habit of learning to feed from the hand but it is a lot smaller than a blackbird, and therefore able to take to the air much more quickly. Since birds use flight as their main defence, and since large birds naturally take longer to become airborne, you would expect that they would be more wary than the smaller ones. I think that this is generally most people's experience, the urban pigeons and ducks of our public parks being the exceptions. The bravery and empathy of my blackbird would seem therefore to be at least the equal of the 'fearless' (rather than perceptive or courageous) robin.

The robin of course, is regarded in Britain as a largely domestic bird, a natural inhabitant of gardens and back yards perhaps because of this very tameness. That perception however is not really true, since the robin is often just as happy, and as common, in the woods and forests, far from any human disturbance. This is why I chose the blackbird to nominate as a domestic familiar. True the sparrow used to be the recognized champion domestic, and even carried that title in its scientific name, Passer domesticus, but sadly the sparrows are not now what they were.

**

The days of my youth when every farmyard and village lane was haunted by the ubiquitous loud and cheerful 'cheeps' as warm and summery as any street trader's chant, seem now to be long gone, though we heard the sound only a few short decades ago. And even more sadly, there seems to be a quite plausible theory that the sparrows' decline is not caused by some great upheaval in farming practises, nature, or the human economy but it may well be that it is simply another victim of the health and safety culture. The spillages of seed, grain and animal feed that were once the sparrows' share, and helped to make them common, are now no more, since even the horses' feed now comes freeze dried in a plastic bag; and for hygiene reasons the farms' grain must be kept in hermetically sealed silos. The days when the ten million hay and oat-fed horses stabled in London, helped gain the sparrow the 'cockney' title, were gone long before even I remember. You can still hear the sparrow now and again of course, but if you want its happy tuneless sound as a permanent background to your summer work and leisure, then those of us who are old enough must listen for it in our hearts, and the young must use their imagination.
You can also make a case for the swifts and martins as domestic house fowl, but although it may be true that they only exist in such great numbers, because we give them their nesting sites beneath our eaves making them dependantly domestic, yet they are only here for the hot days of summer, a holiday romance rather than a true family member.

**

Outside the house window is a small patch of lawn, little used because it serves as a space beside the never-used front door. It is, however, very important to two pairs of local blackbirds, since it marks the much disputed edge of their respective territories. It's possible to sit in the front room window and watch their antics for hours at a time. The two cock birds especially, seem to be obsessed with what my friend calls the 'to and fro' game – where first one cock bird advances, invading the other's personal space, the other retreats until the advancing bird has pushed several feet beyond the invisible boundary line of the territory. Then, having pushed its ambitions as far as it dares, it then loses either its interest or its nerve and turns away. The other male then takes its turn to push the first male back in the same way, and so the game goes on, back and forth across the boundary, for long periods of time. Meanwhile the hen birds hang back, scratching and feeding in the flower borders around the lawns edges, seemingly indifferent to the whole thing. Given that the lawn is a clear open space, after a while it becomes quite possible for even a simple human to work out where the imaginary boundary falls, running in a diagonal line from the old apple tree in one corner to the gate in the other. In consequence while watching the other day I noticed something interesting that I had not realised before, about the occasional fights that occur between the birds, which I think may not be so plain or simple where the terrain is more complex.

Most of the time the 'to and fro' game goes on without any violence, but just occasionally if one of the males loses concentration or is distracted by something, and he finds himself on the wrong side of the other cock – that is to say, further into the opponent's territory than his opponent is – it is then that a fight will almost invariably break out. And it is only then, when a real scrap begins between the males, that the females suddenly join in, rushing over to join in the scrap, and rapidly turning the fight into a furious wing-flapping melée.

However, if you watch closely, you will see that the whole performance is much more structured than it appears at first. Most of the time the males only fight with one another, and the hens are much more intent on fighting their female opponents than they are in scrapping with the males. Often it is only when one of the hens rushes over to help her mate which always seems to arouse the rage of the other, and soon two pairs of birds will rise in the air together, furiously scrabbling at one another. This is behaviour may be quite unusual in any birds but the blackbirds, because I am fairly sure that most female songbirds do not take anything like the same interest in the defence of their territory, or in backing up the mates,

preferring to leave all that entirely to the males.
This little performance was a quite regular display throughout the summer, and could never fail to provide interest to human watchers. Yet it is good to remember that what takes place on the lawn before the windows, is no bitchy squabble between neighbours over suburban trifles, but a real earnest struggle for resources with lives depending on it, though our garden birds may be a source of joy, we are wrong if we smile without a little sadness. Falling out over trifles is a luxury only relatively rich humans can ever afford.

Walls

It's never a good idea to dismiss any location as a potential source of delight, even the most unpromising. Let me explain: when I need to go shopping in our delightful local town, there's one specific little pleasure that's always there, and though that pleasure is small and in the most unexpected place, I should miss it if it was gone.

In the centre of town is a large and relatively dull car park, which since it's only a very small and relatively rustic market town, still offers the amazing treat of free parking, and hopefully, long may that remain so! Having parked my car, I then have a choice of two routes to the main shopping street and the market square, either to go the long way round via a small neat square which contains the post office and a tiny local supermarket, or I may cut through a narrow passage between the buildings. I don't know if this is really a legal right of way, but all the locals seem to treat it as such, and nobody seems to mind.

About halfway down this passage, one of the buildings, which is a little wider than the others, juts out and so the alley narrows. Where this extension joins the other buildings, the angle of the walls create a shady sheltered corner, and for many years an old iron pipe has led down from a gutter two floors above. It must be many years since the rusting old pipe was in any way watertight, and as a consequence the slightly damp wall has grown into a perfect miniature garden.

A long line of plants perhaps two feet wide and ten long, which always seem to be bright and healthy but which never seem to grow more than five or six inches tall, tumble down the wall and wrap round the pipe. It's true there are no great rarities here but it's a good mixed collection none the less, with at least three wall ferns, plus a delicate wall germander which sometimes manages a flower or two to brighten the mini-landscape still further. There's also a much bigger woodland fern which somehow manages to hang on here, only making a fraction of its full size, and finally a tiny delicate carpet of moss mostly towards the bottom.

This wall is only a very minor botanic wonder, nor does it contain anything very rare, yet it's always neat, fresh and pleasing to the eye and well worth a look every time I pass. It's also worth noting that even if the little garden were not pretty, it would still be a remarkable thing that plants in such numbers can thrive on the cold, open, bleak, apparently food-free, and at least occasionally very dry, place.

Not only that, but several of the little plants that grow here, though not rare, are specialists which are hardly ever found growing anywhere else except on walls.

**

Britain possess quite an interesting flora of wall plants which, even only counting the common ones, number several dozen species at least: plants which are more often than not found growing on top of, or in the crevices of man-made walls rather than anywhere else. No doubt, long ago before people started to build walls, these types of plants were confined only to natural cliffs and other rocky outcrops. It's highly likely that they were then nothing like as common as they have been since humans started digging up rocks and minerals in large numbers, and began to build big square piles out of them. In fact, doing just what this particular group of plants needs in order to flourish.

The wall plants would certainly have been rare in this part of lowland England where a natural rock at the surface is virtually unknown. The nearest rocky outcrops to our local town are at least sixty miles away in the South Pennines, which means that this little collection of plants growing on the old wall must be descended from plants whose seeds and spores made their way to here only after humans started to build walls of stone or brick.

Stage by stage little seeds and spores were wafted by the wind from one village wall to the next, leapfrogging across the open spaces, crossing open farmland and the woodlands that barred their way only with the greatest patience and time, waiting for transit on the random services of birds, wind and insects. Until at last they have made their way hundreds of miles from some original and distant enclave in nature's high alpine castles, to every corner of the country where people know how to build. What a migration.

Now that seems wonderful to me. And not only for me but for all people who are in tune with all that is remarkable in the world around them, then surely every such little garden as this is to be treasured. Yet still I wonder just how many people there are who even notice this natural mural, though many must walk past every day. Yet sadly even to concern yourself with such things might be thought by many people to be unusual.

**

One cool summer's day a couple of years ago I went out with some botanist colleagues, as sadly I sometimes do. We spent the whole morning hunting through some local woods and in a very short while found twice as many interesting plants as we had hoped for. Having 'done' the woods by lunchtime, we then had to think of somewhere for the afternoon. We leant on the cars with sandwiches and flasks in hand, enjoying the priceless warmth of some rare sun in what had been a fairly chilly damp summer, and debated the point. I suggested that we should go on to some more woods which I knew of, where there's an unusual combination of plants of the types that are normally found on both acid and lime-rich soils. Such things are usually of great interest to botanists and I thought this should please them well enough. I also pointed out that the drive went through really attractive countryside and ended near to a good place for the evening meal.

One member of the party John, however, wanted to go and look at a wall of which he knew. This was quite a long way off and meant going through a large industrial suburb where little else would be found. He was, in his gentle affable and almost irresistible way, most insistent, and said that the wall was so good that we'd regret it deeply if we never saw it.

He won the day and we set off in convoy following his car. Having passed through the industrial estates, we eventually emerged into one of those small seemingly unhappy little villages that you sometimes find around big towns, who seem to have been left behind by anything approaching planned development, and which still cling to a few acres of green arable and pasture, trapped between the suburbs, the factories and, in this case, the docklands of the river. We stopped on the high street just opposite a lone farm, not quite dead yet but already shrouded by developments, and went over the road to view the wall of an old barn.

Never will I ever regret giving way to John's persuasion that day, because to anyone with an eye for such things the wall was truly spectacular. It was built of rough stone in old lime mortar, and faced north. The old terracotta tiled roof which topped it had no gutters and little overhang; consequently the wall must have been permanently damp, and it grew a crop of wall plants so luxuriant that not a square inch of the stone could be seen. The plants, which were a perfect mix of the familiar and the rare, tumbled down the wall like a lush green waterfall. So dense and rich was the growth that we found it hard to find all the types but when the tally was finally added up we found that none of us could ever remember finding so many species on just one wall, and every single plant growing its heart out, so that it was possible to lose people's faces among the greenery when you tried to photograph the scene.

I was standing back to take a photo when a car pulled out of the yard behind the building; the driver was the farm's owner with his wife beside him. They naturally wound down the window to find out why so many people were standing near their gate. We explained who we were, what we were doing, and that in our opinion, (our group that day contained considerable expertise so its opinion was worth something!) this could well be regarded as perhaps the best wall site in England. The farmer looked for a second or two at the wall as though seeing it for the first time, smiled and said, "What – that?" Then he wound up his window and drove away. I do hope that on reflection he now sometimes notices what he's privileged to own. It would be sad if he didn't, since you don't realy need any great botanical or artistic knowledge to appreciate this sort of natural mural, its beauty alone should be enough.

**

Such appreciation should I think even be taught in our schools, for one of the best known poems of our county poet Alfred Tennyson is addressed to the 'common weeds' found on the wall outside his schoolroom window. This, of course, was back in the nineteenth century when schools could be grim, and small boys would be grateful for a glimpse of something green and growing, however small. And just to prove the persistence that these micro ecosystems can display, that particular wall in our local town, is not only still there nearly two centuries later but still happily has its crop of weeds of just the types that Tennyson describes growing on it, as green and healthy as they ever were.

But sadly that's perhaps a rare thing, for though it's unfortunate that so many people fail to appreciate wall plants, all too often some are actively hostile to them, such unassuming creatures are seen by many as being at least untidy, if not an actual threat to the wall – neither of which is quite true.

Certainly given time, and especially if the walls are not sound to begin with, then the roots of plants can do some damage, slowly leaching and prising, and releasing tiny amounts of softening acid into the bricks and mortar. But the timescales involved are enormous; there's certainly no need to rush out with a chisel and repointing trowel whenever the first tint of chlorophyll green is spotted. In fact the work involved in doing major repairs, if they were ever to become necessary, has got to be less in the long run than all the repeated and obsessive scraping and repointing that seems to be carried out so often in the name of the mindless cult of neatness. Regrettably I know of at least one wall site of great beauty, and at least five different uncommon species which have recently been completely destroyed. The sad thing about this site was that it grew on the side of an old barn high on the plateau of the Wolds, in a location where a little of nature's mellowness could not have been more happily placed. It made the old barn's wall seem at one with all the weathered beauty around and reminding passers-by that even here on so high and bleak a place without soil or shelter, the vigour of life is unquenchable. And I am sorry to say that it was destroyed only as part of a project to give the barn a smart new role in life as a garage for a family car.

Yet perhaps the worst act of vandalism that I ever witnessed was by the wall of a local church; a beautiful modest country church with a tree-filled churchyard where it's always a pleasure to stroll, its walls built of rough old weathered local sandstone with wide mortared joints. One day when reading the gravestones and admiring the spring bulbs, I looked up to see an old lady come round the corner of the church. She stopped by the wall on which were growing a scattering of tiny wall plants, which were certainly no threat to the massive thick walls. She then began slowly carefully and methodically to pull the plants out one at a time, working her way slowly along the wall.

At first I thought that I would try to talk her out of it but then I thought that at her age she was probably beyond redemption, so I said nothing – but in any case it was most unlikely that she would succeed. Wall plants are by their very nature extremely tough and enduring, able to regenerate from the tiniest scrap of root and stem wedged into the smallest crevice. It will not be long in the life of a church before the lady becomes too frail to repeat her vandalism, and then the plants will have this wall to themselves for perhaps centuries to come. Not that I object in any way to people who have a real need to maintain their own domestic spaces but do we really need to apply these actions to an old barn and a country church?

**

But the final twist of irony in all of this is that as I write, I'm living in a country where the very latest in garden fashions is called vertical gardening. For the price of a good small second hand car, you can buy a kit made of plastic and stainless steel components designed to hang on your wall so that you may grow plants on your house. It comes with a strong supporting frame, pockets for the plants, a watering system, (computer controlled of course,) and special growing media. With its help you can turn the walls of your house into fountains of green and flowers, spectacular certainly, if probably a little vulgar in some cases. It is perhaps a very good thing, and I'd love to have one; especially, a realy vulgar expensive one.
But is it not strange that we live in a country where we can spend hundreds of pounds on such a thing, yet can find so little time and effort to even notice, let alone appreciate, what is freely and willingly given by an open-handed nature?

An Acorn Or Two

Sometimes I venture deep into the local forest, to a place where the forestry plantations briefly give way to a little hidden woodland area, light and open with huge mature trees and several large ponds. It is a long way from the main forest track and often thick with midges but worth the effort because here you can find some truly old and massive trees – both oak and Scots pines. Most of them have trunks so wide it would take at least three or four people to link hands around them. The whole place has an air of being primeval and the Forestry Commission seems to have respected it over the years, making no attempt to replant it with commercial trees.

I like to linger there sometimes and enjoy the company of a few things older than me, and most of the time the dog is content to let me slow down awhile because it's a good place for her to indulge in her passion for squirrel watching. Yet I have to admit that however good the trees are as company, the feeling of being in a place that is ancient and changeless is probably just an illusion. Not least because the oaks and pines, although they're British natives, are almost certainly plantings, neither being a common 'wildings' in Lincolnshire, and the whole, judging from its overall layout, was once no doubt part of the ornamental plantings of some long gone estate.

According to legend there was once a time, before humans began to deforest the land, when the whole of Britain was covered from one shore to the other with a single large forest of oaks trees, with perhaps an under-story of its close partner and disciple, the hazel. One of the more commonly heard lighthearted versions of the legend tells that, so dense and complete was the cover, a squirrel could cross the whole country from one side to the other without touching the ground. The story is no more than a gross oversimplification and I don't think that anyone could ever have believed it even approached within a country mile of literal truth. Many modern historians have cast real doubts on the density of the supposed canopy, suspecting that in parts the primeval woodland may well have been quite open with many wide sunny glades. However, the influence of this particular myth could well hide from many people another important truth about the ecology of early Britain, which is just how diverse the tree cover of the untouched wilderness really was.

Most people may be aware that Scots pine and birch woods probably took over from the oaks in the far north, but that fact alone

by no means completes the picture. For example, here in my home county of Lincolnshire, there is good evidence that woods of lime trees predominated over large areas, especially in the central lowlands. Moreover it should also be remembered that in early prehistory, much of the country would often have consisted of un-drained marshland, which was probably covered either by reeds or quite often by willow or alder woods; usually known as 'Carr'.
I suspect that here in the north east (where ash is very much the main hedgerow tree today) ash woods may well have been the norm in some places, even in pre-human times, just as they were in much of Scandinavia. Some yew woods are also believed to be ancient, and while even though they may never have formed true forests, there must have been areas where, aided by local soil and climate, other common trees like elms and beeches at least formed woods occasionally, though chestnut at least, may be an introduction.
Of course Britain was never covered from one end to another with one solid block of oak wood; at best there was a rich patchwork quilt of forest cover, mingling from place to place and changing over time. Nor was the oak forest all of one type because Britain has at least two native oaks, each of which has a quite distinct character and range. They still linger in pretty much in their original niches today, and if you wish to indulge in a little botany it's both easy and amusing to tell them apart.

**

The slightly commoner of the two, and the typical tree of 'Old England', is Quercus robur, or the Pedunculate Oak, while in the west and north west, especially in the mountains of Wales and on high ground generally, the Sessile Oak, or Quercus petraea, is more commonly found. It's well worth the effort needed to distinguish between them because they're quite different in character, as are their soil requirements, should you wish to plant them. And they're certainly not hard to tell apart or remember, since this is a rare case where the common or English names give you better botany than the Latinised binaries do. 'Pedunculate' simply means 'stalked' and this refers to the seeds or acorns that hang away from the twigs on long slender stems. On the other hand, 'Sessile' is an Anglicised form of Latin meaning 'close' or 'un-stalked', and indeed the cups which hold the acorns are attached close to the twigs.
So it really is that easy. Well no, of course not, it's never quite that

easy because there are just two small wrinkles that could lead to confusion. The first of which is that the pedunculate and sessile qualities refer solely to the acorns and not to the leaves which, just to be perverse, have exactly the opposite qualities. Those of the Sessile Oak are quite stalked, the leaves of the pedunculate cling closely to the twigs. However, in some ways that is in itself quite helpful because if you only remember that the leaves show the opposite habits to the seeds then you'll be able to tell even young immature plants apart. And the quirkiness of that anomaly does help you remember your facts quite easily, does it not? Especially now that I've annoyed you with it!

The other small difficulty is that the two trees breed together so that there are intermediate plants and you can therefore only put them into rough groupings but there are many more pure bred trees than hybrids; and if you can tell them apart even basically then you gain a valuable insight because the whole character of the plants are so different. Quercus robur is tall and stately – the great spreading oak of the deep shaded forest, ideal for planting where the rainfall is low and the soil is deep. The Quercus petraea is full of gritty character - often twisted and shaggy with lichen, it looks, even when in deep woodland, as if it were made for clinging to high stony ground in wild mountain gorges.

The difference is also important if you wish to plant an oak. You might think that there are few people left with the space to do this now, but if you have only a reasonably sized garden you could, if you wished, still plant the iconic tree, as there are several smaller forms, including an upright growing, or so-called 'fastigiate' form.

**

Especial care must be taken in the choice of oak to be planted if you live on a lime-rich or chalky soil. Our village is perched high on the Lincolnshire Wolds and has a very lime rich soil, which created a slight problem when it came to the Millennium. The village school wanted to plant a commemorative tree to mark the notable occasion, and of course the first choice of tree for such an occasion had to be an oak.

Unfortunately the school and its playing fields are on the higher slopes above the valley base where the soil is exceptionally thin, little more than a skimming of dirt over a hundred metres or more of solid chalk. However the greatest care was taken with the choice of

plants, making really sure that we got the true lime-resistant Quercus robur, and not any crossbred plant, some of which do not have Q robur's lime tolerance. We succeeded however, and I'm pleased to report that the tree thrives and grows to this day (2016) despite extensive building work taking place all around it.
Yet for all that, the general perception is that oaks may seem to be difficult and overlarge for modern gardens and even outdated in today's world. This is perhaps because while we generally think of 'the oak' as a singular thing, usually Quercus robur, there are, in fact, very few genera of trees which even approach the size or diversity of the oaks, with some forty or so species grown in this country alone. Moreover, oaks are a genera which is widespread across both the old and new worlds, with species numbered in three figures, and which vary from evergreen plants with silvered glossy leaves in the hot dry semi-desert regions of the sub tropics, to the tall thick limbed giant of the deep northern forests.
All of them, however, are easy to recognise by their characteristic seeds or acorns, carried semi-enclosed in the familiar neat little cups. Given their widespread nature and diversity, this way of bearing seeds is obviously very successful, and there is no doubt that there are many animals, from jays and crows to the industrious squirrels, that are grateful for the natural harvest and busy for long hours gathering and hiding the seeds of the many species of oaks.

**

Each year for many years now The Fern Nursery has attended a number of horticultural and agricultural shows, where we construct displays designed to advertise and sell the plants we grow. These displays are also judged and prizes awarded, and therefore since our plants are mostly the inhabitants of shade, we try to set them off to best effect by building a miniature woodland landscape on the bench top, where our plants appear to grow naturally among the moss and leaves.
One year we met the judge after the show who said he was very impressed by the display but where, in early September, had we managed to obtain the dry autumn leaves which were scattered on the spaces between the plants as if they had just fallen from the trees. I explained that the leaves were a year old, and that it was my habit to go out each autumn and collect several baskets-full of newly

fallen leaves which are then stored in a shed until needed. This seemed to amuse him greatly and he thought it an act of considerable foresight and endeavour on my part. In truth it's mainly a pleasure since collecting autumn leaves on a dry sunny day at the fading end of the year is not only a pleasant pursuit but also one of thrift that suits my northern nature! Leaves which are there for the collecting are a lot cheaper than other natural products such as composted bark or sphagnum moss which cost large sums of money when bought in tidy plastic bags from the wholesaler.

My tree of choice for the collecting expedition is the American Red Oak, Quercus rubar, which grows in a woodland a couple of miles away. The leaves of red oak are truly beautiful, being much larger than those of our native species and often have a reddish tint which in part accounts for the tree's name. Moreover they dry well into large crispy flakes of brown leather, keeping well for several years and making them ideal for displays.

The keeping quality is probably because most species of oak are especially rich in tannins and other preservative chemicals. This is why in the past oak bark was widely used as a preservative – large amounts for example, being used in tanneries for the production of leather. The new hides were put to soak in huge vats filled with oak bark until the skins become completely infused with the antibiotic chemicals in the bark. So high is the tannin content that in the past a use was also found for making ink, since tannin reacts with iron to yield a dark blue dye.

The parts most used for the ink-making purpose were not leaves, bark or acorns or any other natural organ of the tree but the small growths often found on some twigs, called oak apples. The so-called 'apples' have nothing to do with fruiting but are growths produced by the trees in reaction to an attack by a small parasitic wasp, though they do look very like small spherical fruits about the size of a crab apple. Naturally the tree, being under attack, concentrates its tannins in the area of the growth which is what made the small 'galls' as they are properly called, so useful in the past as a source of chemicals.

Oak trees suffer from a huge range of attackers and parasites. It is perhaps because they were once so common that they became the number one source of food and shelter for many creatures, quite a lot of which have now become completely wedded to the oaks and can now live on nothing else; this may well account for the exceptional strength of the oaks' chemical defences. It also provides a very persuasive reason for planting them, because by its very nature every oak tree is effectively a miniature nature reserve on a stalk, supporting not only a vast range of invertebrate parasites but also all the creatures, especially small birds, which feed on those invertebrates.

Red oak is an easy tree to grow, and well worth the space if you have it. Not only are the leaves large and handsome – new spring growth has a bright colour and good autumn colour – but the tree also has a fine upright shape with fast growth. If you are minded towards conservation, it's true that no trees support anything like the wildlife that the native British oaks do but even so the Red Oak is still far better than many foreign trees you could plant.

**

As well as autumn leaves, there's another even more important and interesting ingredient which we use in our show bench displays: cork. Cork – the very same stuff you pull out of your bottle of wine – is yet another product of the amazingly helpful and varied oak genera. The cork used in wine bottles is generally of better quality, while for the shows we use whole long rolls of second grade material up to six feet long. When these are arranged carefully on the bench top and surrounded by plants, moss, leaves and other natural materials, they look almost exactly like fallen logs, yet they weigh no more than a tenth of the of the weight of real timber.

Cork is no more than the outer bark of a Mediterranean oak, the Cork Oak, Quercus suber, which has been peeled off the trunk and the larger branches in hollow rolls or tubes that are split down one side and open at the ends. Because the cork oak grows in semi-open habitats under the hot dry Mediterranean sun, its bark is especially thick and waterproof for protection, which is what makes it such a useful and versatile material.

The bark is harvested in the spring from trees that are at least 25 years old, by people called 'extractors' who peel it off using axes and knives. It can then be harvested again every nine or ten years or so because the really amazing thing is that harvesting the bark in this way does the trees little harm and they can go on living and growing for perhaps three hundred years. This is remarkable because usually peeling the bark off the majority of trees, especially round the trunk, will quite quickly kill most of them. This is because the bark forms a protective layer, which prevents the layer of the trunk called 'vascular tissue' (which carries water and minerals around the tree) from drying out or bleeding the tree to death. To a gardener at least, the whole business seems counter-intuitive because bark ringing a tree is usually recommended as a good way to kill one, particularly if you have a need to do so and can't cut it down completely. Yet it seems that the Cork Oak has both an outer and an inner bark which, at one particular time of the year in late spring and early summer, will separate, leaving the inner bark behind intact and able to protect the tree.

**

Recently we had the chance to visit Portugal which is the main centre of the cork trade, at the time of year when the bark had been collected, and were delighted to find that, although a large scale industry, the cork trade is still delightfully informal. It may be that in parts of Portugal the cork plantations are formally laid out and of large scale, but in the southern hills which we visited there was no such organisation. Most of the cork trees seemed to grow out in the semi-wild in an informal way, but many more simply grew in orchards and back yards beside the road and alongside other trees in odd ones and twos. Yet behind the trade somewhere, there is a high standard of control needed, because the trees are harvested systematically and marked with numbers after harvest, to make sure they are never over-cropped.

Cork Oak plantations and the wild to semi-wild habitat that surround them, are an important part of the economy around much of the Mediterranean and the Iberian peninsular. They provide a serious economic return which helps to maintain a lot of land in a state where much of the natural Mediterranean flora, and all the wildlife which goes with it, is still allowing them to flourish on a large scale undisturbed, except by a person with an axe for a short hour every decade or so.

However, in the last few years there has been a crisis in the cork industry as many wine producers turned away from traditional corks in favour of screwtops and artificial corks, which has led to a serious threat to the cork oak industry and the traditional habitat.

In response, the cork producers are tackling the threat to their traditional industry in two ways: in part by trying to hold on to their traditional trade by taking a marketing strategy which emphasises the green nature of natural corks in wine bottles, their low carbon footprint, biodegradable nature, and the environmental benefits of cork. But also by finding an increasing number of alternative uses for what is a truly versatile natural material, so that you can now find everything from shoes and handbags, to floor tiles, book bindings and even umbrellas, all made from an amazingly strong flexible and durable natural material.

The cork trade seems genuinely to be pushing hard to raise the profile of its new products; you can see exhibits of cork products all over Portugal and on the internet. Whether any of these new items will prove to be long-term winners, and if the cork producers can persuade the world to keep pulling bits of the Mediterranean-rich flora out of the necks of their wine bottles, is still up in the air but I for one, having seen the natural wonders of Iberia, will now look carefully at the stopper next time I buy a bottle of wine.

You'd find it hard to grow the Cork Oak in Britain but some of the Mediterranean oaks will grow quite well even this far north in the UK, including the other common wild species of the dry south, the Evergreen or Holm Oak. The Holm Oak makes a wonderfully large tree for a park or estate, though it can only be grown in smaller gardens if it is kept regularly clipped but it's a first class plant for topiary and withstands the pruning well. This is the way it's commonly used in the gardens of the Mediterranean, where pruned evergreens are the staple plants in every garden, fulfilling the southern need for both shade and summer greenery.

The Holm Oak also shows a curious feature in that it has two different sorts of leaves. At the top of the tree, and for the most part in mature trees, you will find glossy spindle shaped leaves, while in young plants, and at lower levels especially, the leaves are spiky, like small holly leaves, which is the character which gets it the third of its common names, being sometimes called Holly Oak, or Quercus ilex.

**

Once when young, I was sent by a customer to buy some plants of Holm Oak and when I arrived in the nursery, I was offered some young plants with the typical holly-like leaves. Being only familiar with the plant as a mature tree, I then entered into a dispute with the nurseryman over whether I was being offered the correct plant or not. Fortunately I took them and the customer who presumably knew better, was quite happy. But when I realised the foolish mistake, I spent a number of youthful years hoping that the nurseryman would forgive me the time wasted. Since then though, I've become a nursery owner myself, and now realise that nurserymen have twenty such conversations a week, so he probably forgot about it within the hour.

The spiky leaves are most probably an adaptation to help the plant defend itself against browsing. Many trees and shrubs show a similar habit, such as our common hawthorn, which in some strains has large numbers of thorns at a level of the reach of animals, and is then often quite free of them higher up. Yet in very few trees is the change quite so dramatic as it is in the Holm Oak, where the two leaf forms are quite different. And the good thing is that the spiny holly-like leaves are encouraged even more by clipping, so that small managed plants will often have an attractive appearance quite unlike that of most oaks. There is though just one small catch to planting Holm Oak in small gardens, which is that if you sell the house and garden, then you must remember to tell the new owners to keep up the clipping, because a mature Holm Oak is a truly huge tree, with a heavy deep shade. Just the sort of thing you would want spreading its cool embrace over your cottage under the baking sun of a Mediterranean summer, but not what you'd want in a British winter!

Waterside

The pond, especially when it's in the full growth of summer, is one of the main signs of the moving seasons, since more than any other part of the garden the summer pond is a very different place to the pond in winter; the lush and rapid growth of the pond side plants narrowing it from being as wide as perhaps twelve feet in February, to as little as a couple of feet of clear water in June. In part of course this is simply because of the easy access waterside plants have to ample moisture which enables them to make the sort of rapid soft foliage growth in the spring which plants growing in drought prone soils can't.

That this is so is perhaps obvious to most people, but there's more to it than that, and what makes the change seem even more dramatic is the fact that while many waterside plants make a lot of growth in summer, they also die down completely in the winter, making the pond side one of the barest parts of the garden in the cold weather. The reason for this is clearly (if not scientifically) proven that since waterside habitats are always prone to winter flooding, it follows that if plants were to carry a lot of foliage in winter then they would be liable to be damaged, washed away or drowned. Or at the very least their leaves would be caked in mud and sliced in half by ice, which would render them pretty useless to the plant; therefore it pays the waterside plant to pull its nose in when winter arrives.

I had always thought that this would be obvious to most people but over the years I've been in the gardening trade, I've been repeatedly surprised by the number of people who have come to me and quite innocently expressed disappointment at the limited range of evergreens that are available for growing in wet places – it seemingly coming as a complete surprise to them that there could be a reason why this should be so.

**

In modern times ponds, rivers and canals are often made with plastic, clay, fibreglass or even concrete linings, and frequently fitted with overflows, which means that the ground even a few feet from the water's edge may be quite dry all year round. People who garden beside such artificial wetlands are therefore able to grow almost anything they wish. However, the rivers and streams which we most often visit and treasure for their beauty are usually those in hilly places where the ground slopes steeply, and it may well be that the familiarity of such plant groupings blinds people to the fact that in most temperate lowlands it's rare in nature to see evergreens, and especially tall ones, by the waterside.

There are though a few exceptions, (to the plants as well as the people!). Some of the horsetails such as Equisetum varigata, and E. japonicum stay green through winter and like the waterside, as do a few ferns such as Blechnums. Then there are a couple of bamboos, blueberries or Vacciniums, and some Iris stay leafy for quite a while; and in mild areas, New Zealand Flax, plus a few others that don't come to mind right now. But it's hardly a long list, and in the end if you have a wet spot in the garden perhaps it's best just to embrace the drama of the seasons as nature intended it, rather than fight for something that may just end up looking tired and scruffy.

The old advice given, which was once a cliché of the garden books, though I've not seen it reiterated so often recently, was that you should never put water features near to windows because of their poor effects in winter. Perhaps this was because it was thought you shouldn't have something grey and lifeless by your windows in winter. Or maybe, as urban legend had it, it was felt that cold grey water with no plants to soften it in the damp and dismal season would act as a gardeners' diuretic, sending the viewer running from the window to the toilet. Who knows?

A gentle plea for the art of weeding

You could not make a better start than with something basic, truly down among the grass roots, and weeding is just that, if anything, the Cinderella of all the gardening crafts. I suspect that it's simply considered by many gardeners to be little more than an irksome task which must be endured now and again before you can move on to the really interesting stuff, like planting, propagating or even pruning. It seems therefore almost an embarrassment to have to say this but to my mind if there could ever be just one good and outstanding reason for possessing a garden, then it must be because it enables you to practise the art of weeding.

This may be of course, just a freaky personal quirk, and if you know me, then you'll know that I have a more than my fair share of quirks, especially the sort which have a way of annoying other people. But please read on, because this one at least, may be just a little bit less annoying than most.

I don't think that anyone, even the least enthusiastic weeder, would say that weeding isn't important. We all realise that since nature always all too willingly gives back ten thousand fold or more for every one that is pulled out, then all gardens are much more a product of what we take out than by the tiny fraction which we put back in. Indeed if weeding is defined as the removal of unwanted plant matter (and it easily could be) then dividing, pruning and cutting back are also in their own way, types of weeding. Which would make weeding virtually all that the art of gardening consisted of; like a sculpture, a garden is made much more by what you remove than by what you put in. So perhaps it's best if we set out in the spirit of, 'We're really going to enjoy and make the most of this'.

**

Think for a minute about what happens when you enter a border with a fork in your hand, when you've really got your nose down among the leaves. Do you not then become more intimate with your garden than at any other time? Do you ever get closer to your plants than this? Not only that, but isn't it true that you see and understand even more at this time than any other – at least because this is when you are most actively intervening in the natural ecology of your garden. You'll see which plant runs under which, how each plant

spreads, how its roots extend, with what weeds it competes, and to which it gives way, how high the crowns form, when the buds come through the spring soil and so much more.
Not only that, but you'll learn huge amounts about the weeds themselves, which are only wild flowers after all, from when they come through to what their seed, leaves and roots look like, and this in turn will often tell you much about their cultivated relatives. If there's any single gardening activity which has taught you as much about plants or nature as weeding has, then I would be very pleased to know about it and have a go.
Perhaps we tend to under value all this knowledge, partly because we take it for granted, since it's gained as a 'freebie' along with a tidy garden, but even more perhaps because there's simply so much of it, and so painlessly gained, that we could never hope to organise it all in our minds or write it down. But what about remembering the joy of learning just for its own sake? Why should those of us who are gardeners ever forget just how impressed non-gardeners sometimes are by the fact that we can always tell a plant from a weed, (well nearly always!) and isn't that a really true measure of just how far and how near to the earth weeding has brought you?
Then again, if we're seeking the joys of weeding, what many and various ways there are – let me just think a second. There's forking out, digging in, the hoe (both push and pull), mulching, herbicide and hand pulling at least. Something in fact to suit every weather and mood, and you can probably think of a few more. I strongly suspect that a lot of the unenthusiastic weeders you encounter fall into one of the puritanical method schools of weeding, as in, "Keep the hoe going all the time, I want to have loose earth and clear space between all my plants at all times and never mind the seedlings." Well that's their loss, at the very least because picking and planning a strategy to suit each challenge is all part of the fun.
For a warm relaxing summer's day in the sunshine when you're feeling mellow, then hoeing is not only at its most effective then but it can be done with an upright posture, covering the ground quickly and soon achieving that special feeling of satisfaction you need before you can allow yourself a little time for sitting at the bottom of the garden in the shade with a drink.
(The hoe, incidentally is a hook, and which should be slightly blunt, used to pull the weeds from the ground, leaving them on the surface with roots and leaves still joined, that way they wilt and die much quicker. It should never be used to slice the tops off weeds leaving

the roots behind. I know that many of you know better but I've seen the wrong method advocated by – naturally you guessed it! – a well-known TV presenter. So I thought it needed a mention.)

And when you've finished your drink, you can work your way back up the garden and turn them over again, just to make sure and give yourself an extra little sadistic thrill. Do also try one of the newfangled 'push and pull' hoes – you may like it.

Mulch is, of course, good exercise on a cold winter's day, when the ground is hard with frost and your breath steams. But it's also fun to use it opportunistically. Do you have a barrow full of spent compost to get rid of? Ah, just the thing! Dump it on those weed seedlings. Double the satisfaction.

Hand weeding with a fork is naturally the connoisseurs' method; slow and fulfilling, it achieves the closest intimacy with both plant and earth. It may not be the best of ways with some running weeds, but it certainly feels like it, especially when you peel a long slender root in one complete piece from the ground. Ideal for a misty autumn morning with a few crispy fallen leaves lodged around the plants, and a mood of soft melancholy. It keeps you low and out of the wind, and it should be interrupted every hour for a hot drink; and naturally as often as you like for a contemplative pause.

**

Weedkiller is quick and convenient, as well as the only way with some weeds. Always use a sprayer with a trigger on the lance, and a flat fan pattern nozzle, never a mist nozzle. If you're worried about splashing your plants, then you're using the wrong equipment. If you're spraying small weeds between plants, then there's no need to lift the nozzle more than three or four inches off the ground; you should in fact be able to use herbicide to thin trays of seedlings. Herbicide is only a weapon of mass destruction in the hands of clumsy and oafish members of the opposite sex, (insert your own choice of gender here). Do check the weather forecast and don't be afraid to use a second/third/fourth dose on tough weeds if they prove rebellious.

Herbicide is by no means a new technology; the Ancient Romans probably used salt to keep the paths clear in their villa gardens. In fact the Romans seem to have been addicted to salt, using it as a cleaner, an antiseptic, a disinfectant, and to clean themselves after they had been to the toilet; they even added huge amounts to their food. I would think that in the garden they most probably used it on their gravel areas, in paving cracks, to keep moss off tiles, to discourage slugs, to kill deep rooted weeds and to clean and sterilise their frames and greenhouses, if they had any. They probably just put their gloves on and scattered handfuls where they needed to. They would of course need to use it with great care near the roots of trees and on areas which were to be planted, as it does spread and persist in the soil a little. The salt they most probably used would be just like the common sort of rock salt that you can buy in bags from the builders' merchant, meant for clearing ice from the drive in winter and which is usually sold at a tiny fraction of the price of herbicides from the garden centre. I can't of course instruct you today to use salt as a weed killer because that wouldn't be legal, as the law says that the product needs to be licensed at great cost for use as a herbicide, which that sort of salt is not, and I would also have to be licensed at great cost, to advice you. So I'm merely contenting myself by telling you what the Romans may have done...

**

Hand pulling without the aid of tools is, as I'm sure you're well aware, possible with many weeds, especially on light soils and when the ground is moist. Some people are violently opposed to this method, "It will break and you'll leave the roots behind". But the experienced and sensitive gardener soon learns to recognise which weeds are susceptible to this method and which are not. The big advantage of this method is that it is the ultimate in opportunistic weeding, you can do it anywhere and any time. I make a point of never walking round the garden without paying for my enjoyment, if I can, by pulling out at least three weeds.
What however is surprising is just how useful this sort of occasional hand weeding is when, in being repeated so regularly you can soon destroy an awful lot of weeds, and since you often tend to get the weeds that you miss when you're doing more organised weeding, (especially those little seedlings which lurk in corners) you can often catch them before they become a menace. The problem with this is, of course, what to do with the weeds when you've pulled them up, as it may be a long way to the compost heap. What I like to do is to place them carefully among the stems of a plant, off the ground, where they're sure to wilt whatever the weather. The bonus of this method is that it greatly annoys some people who will tell you that

the whole garden will soon become filled with hay, but as the weeds are small, quickly wilt, and the plants they're placed on usually grow, you'll never really see them again.

No, the real problem with this method of weeding, and indeed some of the others, is that it can become very obsessive. That special feeling of satisfaction which comes from being able to stand back and think in bellicose metaphors such as 'that's got the little blighters on the run'. In short the feeling that by sheer persistence you're gaining ground over determined resistance, is one of the most addictive things I know, and it can soon lead to you wanting nothing else, but remember even gardeners need a social life sometimes!

Herbs

When young and easily seduced I fell completely in love (as most young gardeners do at least for a little while), with herbs. It isn't difficult to understand why this particular group of plants has such a ready hold on a young mind; simply because those which are generally known in English as 'herbs' are not in any way a natural group of plants, being merely a sweeping conglomerate made up from nearly as many different botanical groups as it's possible to find. The only thing that connects them is the fact that they're the plants which we human beings make the most uses of, at least if you remove the staple food plants from the list.

It's therefore no surprise that this very varied and rather seductive group feeds the gardeners' collecting urge, for not only do they have a wide range of practical uses but also a far richer treasury of human associations than almost any other plant group, with a seemingly unlimited store of epic stories and sheer romance.

Sadly, of course, the fine pleasures of early obsession often lead eventually to a revulsion as deep as the obsession was lofty, and in truth I must confess that I fell out of love with herbs. To a certain degree the culture of herbs is in many ways backward looking, and when you're young and eager, the romance of this soon wears off, especially as you reach that age when you want to put anything associated with the past, (including the embarrassment of earlier loves), far behind you.

Yet tolerance eventually comes with age if not maturity, and as there are many very real pleasures to be found in the herb garden, you would lose much if you continued to hold a youthful prejudice past its proper time. And it therefore came to a point where I felt a return trip to the herb nursery was needed.

**

For many years I've known a herb garden which is also a small nursery, both of them owned for most of that time by a lady of great wisdom, sunny manner and splendid appearance, who runs the nursery and garden in a way that was entirely her own. There was little hint of marketing sophistication there, the nursery is innocent of even a car park, you must park on the wild grass verges by the side of a country road.

Like all the best gardens, it's entered though a little wooden gate beneath an arch, that creaks pleasantly as you go in. To me, whatever the pleasures to be found within a garden, they're nearly always doubled if there's a proper ritual of entrance to mark your rite of passage from the outside world. When once you've entered, the garden proves to be quite small and enclosed, and there's hardly any space to separate the garden and the nursery, with potted plants for sale all jumbled together among those growing in the borders in a happy sort of chaos nearly as artless as nature herself. Yet among the randomness there are great riches tucked into every corner, reflecting the wide diversity of the herbs themselves. Here you can find Umbellifers and Compositaes, some of the most advanced of modern plants which are as sophisticated, swift, harsh and remorselessly efficient as only the truly modern can be. Yet they're growing close beside, and obligingly throwing their protective shade over Equisetums, plants so old in their deeply grooved unchanging habits that they really deserve the title of living fossils, and would get that proud honour if they weren't already better known to everyone as 'them horrible weeds'.

It's one of the great benefits of herbs that many of them would be considered weeds but for their histories or practical usefulness. This happy chance, however, manages to buy for them – despite their poor manners and plebeian associations – the odd place in even the best gardens. Many plants, herbs included, would never find a place in the worst of gardens if they were only valued on conventional lines, so that hopefully our gardens, and also our appreciation of what is good and beautiful, gains in richness because of them. For instance, would plants like Angelica and Lovage, huge perennials with large dramatic leaves, but only greenish white or greenish yellow flowerheads made of many small florets clustered together, find a place in our gardens if they weren't grown first as herbs? Or likewise would the modest little Thyme, with its tiny leaves and short stature, have received the breeding needed to produce so many dozens of cultivars, often with coloured leaves of silver and gold, if it hadn't been a kitchen herb?

Yet when we do find a place in the garden for them, how soon do these plants find a way into our affections, and how loath we would then be, to be without them. And so you visit the herb nursery and browse through the many strange little corners beneath shrubs, behind greenhouses and down little brick paths, poking and leisurely gleaning to find the plants you want among mixtures of pots that are completely undisciplined by botany or alphabets. It's remarkable, though, that they still seem to know, like wild plants or by some hidden wisdom, how to find their rightful homes by sun and shade, wind and water, with many of them escaping into the crevices and gaps beneath the walls where they grow untroubled by hoes or customers.

But having found your plants, you're not by any means finished with all that the little herb nursery has to offer, for when you've toured the delightful but tiny garden and picked out the rare treasures that you must have, you'll still have the entertaining task of paying for them. Strange though it sounds, this may well be an even greater pleasure than the ones you've enjoyed so far, because in order to pay for your plants you must venture into the drying room.

**

On the back of the house is an extension with a sloping roof. Not a modern addition to the house but an old part of the building built out of ancient brick with a traditional tiled roof. I would guess that it was once the dairy or store room but now it's become the heart of the business, being used for selling the plants, as well as drying and storing the cut herbs, and a shop for the herbal products that are produced here. The room is cool and dim when you step in from the sunshine, with polished wooden floors and small bright windows high in the south wall. But as your eyes adjust to the dim interior you soon realise that the room is quite in character with the garden outside, being a rich jumbled chaos of storage jars, sheaves of hanging plants drying naturally, and old lovingly restored wooden cabinets filled with deep drawers, each of which is stuffed full to the brim with the preserved wealth of the garden. Only the owner knows her way through this confusion, and her experienced hands are able to conjure an answer to any request without ever resorting to a treasure map.

Inevitably, though, it's the smell more than anything that impresses, mostly because it's not even remotely like the sadly familiar and completely synthetic herbal aroma that clings chokingly and oppressively about so many tourist attraction gift shops. No, the smell here is far richer, deeper and more earthy, and it draws you in, making you want to smell again and again, and each time that you do so, taking another step forward, you find yet another distinct smell, sometimes familiar garden flowers, and sometimes rich mixtures of little known herbs and spices blending happily together.

The owner, however, takes a special delight in making you smell more, opening jars and inviting you to dip your nose delightedly, then marshalling you along to smell some more with her pet phrase of, "If you liked that, just try this." Eventually you begin to think that in a place like this even the bricks and roof tiles must be odorous. Yet in the end all smells fade with repeated use until finally just one soft lingering perfume remains which seems to stay the distance, no matter how long you've been standing in the shop. A soft faint scent of new mown hay, perhaps the most basic of all floral scents and the very essence of the summer meadow, trapped by drying to last the winter through.

And what an incredible range of herbs there is here in this little space, not just herbs for the kitchen or herbs to cure and revive, but herbs to clean, to polish, to scent your house or your clothes, to make your garden grow and even to make love with. And what a range of products there are – dried herbs of course but also powdered and ground, made into lotions, dissolved in oil, sown into all manner of craft products and boiled into sweets, in fact something to suit all of human life is here.

Of course you always leave having bought more than you came for, and that alone is a rare experience if like me, you're Yorkshire born and Lincolnshire raised. I don't know if any of the herbal mixtures that the owner prescribes to the people who come to her with their ailments work or not – fortunately I've never needed them but I would think that if you did, then just a visit to her shop was enough to work more than half the cure.

The Winter Garden

It is a tired cliché beloved of gardening books when they're being smug and clever, to say that you should plan your garden for the winter and let the summer take care of itself. The old worn argument goes that the garden will always look good in the summer anyway, and as winter occupies half the year, it's therefore wasteful to plan your garden for only the six summer months, when you could be out there getting the benefit for twelve. Well in the last few years, especially as I now garden mainly for summer visitors, I've been coming to the conclusion that while there maybe some truth in this, as a whole it simply just doesn't add up.

Firstly because the winter isn't six months. The gardener's autumn, as we all know, stretches till late November at least, and the spring really starts in March, if not even earlier. So that real winter lasts just three months at most. But having said that, it is in terms of the real 'garden enjoyment time' that winter is so short. If you take off the days when the weather is too foul to get out, the days when you don't get home until dark, (especially if you work), and the days when the garden is under snow – when even mine looks brilliant – just how much time is left for the enjoyment of winter planting? So why lose any of your summer display for something that is essentially ephemeral and we may only enjoy for less than an hour each year. Nor do I think that trying to artfully banish the winter is a good thing anyway. Surely the best thing of all that a garden can give us is that it should truly celebrate the seasons, all of them.

For these reasons I'm now coming to think that if I take up garden space for winter plants only, then they have to be really good, and I mean very Good with a capital 'G', and that they should truly be winter plants, not merely summer plants engineered to have longer seasons. Nor am I looking for any subtlety in winter. In the summer I'll happily join you in admiring the gray-blue bloom on a gray-green leaf if only because subtlety really isn't by any means the predominant theme in summer. But in winter when the East wind blows cold sleet down my ears, a good Lincolnshire squelch creeps over my boots and there are gray stems and soft bark tones in abundance, then what I want and need is fireworks and carnivals. And so I can well do without plants like Winter Sweet, for the poor washed-out colours just aren't strong enough, however good the scent may be. (I have a poor nose.) Also a good winter plant must have a long season because if the week contains only a couple of hours good light and good weather on a Friday, then a plant that starts on Monday and is over by Wednesday is no use at all. But fortunately since all things, including both gardeners and their plants, move more slowly in winter, most of the winter flowers do have a very long season, though there are a few winter/early spring flowers that are all too brief. Beautiful as it is, and it is indeed breathtaking, I'm always disappointed by the Blood Root, Sanguinaria canadensis, where even the double form, which is said to last longer than the single, can still barely manage to last a week at most.

**

However in the garden now as I write, (20th March) there is a Hamamelis, Witch Hazel, which has flowered powerfully for three months, and is only just beginning to fade to a tawny gold, a colour perhaps even better now in fading than the full bloom. Now that's truly is a long season, giving really good value for the space it occupies even if, as some people say it's dull in summer, though the bush has a good goblet form and pleasant soft hairy leaves and stems even in the growing season. Likewise many of the spring bulbs are the most popular of winter plants, precisely because they give a burst of brightness for such a long time. Snowdrops can last six weeks or more and there are bound to be some pleasant days in that time – and with snowdrops it's the really intense whiteness that is part of the attraction.
For which reason I can't say that I'm really a great a fan of Helleborus niger, the black hellebore, the washed out white just seems so sad on a winter's day. Yes you can blanch them to make a better white but that means either lifting them when they stop being a garden flower, or filling the garden with covers, neither of which really improves the winter garden. I would much prefer to use that space for H. hybridus types, preferably in a decent pink, spotted or true green and white, not a subtle 'brown purple greenish puce', not for my tastes anyway. Nor would I underrate any of the green flowered hellebores at this time of the year, when fresh green can be rare; and how they do last, for months on end.
Of the bulbs and corms, to my mind only Iris unguicularis, Stinking Iris, and the common Winter Aconite can really rival the Snowdrop. But since most winter bulbs tend to be small and undemanding of garden space, there is therefore little lost by planting however many we wish. Yes I know the aconites spread everywhere but how often

do you see robust summer flowers overwhelmed by them? For that precise reason however, I find it is hard to place, or find any affection for Iris foetidissima, the foliage is so intrusively ugly all year round, it seems an enormous price to pay for a few winter berries, especially as the foliage is often at its ugliest and most intrusive in the winter, when we have little else, and I feel that this cancels out much of the pleasure the berries may bring.

**

Then there's another common cliché that you should plant mainly evergreens close to the house, because it's said the garden in winter is mainly viewed from the dwelling windows. There may be some truth in this but a lot of evergreens are in many ways at their least exciting in winter. Even those people who don't have a prejudice against conifers for example, must recognise that these plants are really at their best in summer, displaying their fresh new growth and buds, and much the same applies to hollies and other shrubs. Moreover evergreens cut out more of the scarce winter sun than we usually want, making for a dark and dank outlook in winter even if not in summer. And anyway there's surely a case for celebrating the real strengths of winter, and what could be more seasonal than viewing bare stems lit by the low winter sun shining through?
Why not instead plant something like my Hamamelis near the windows with winter bulbs beneath – it will let through lots of light in winter and the bulbs will thrive. Then in summer the ground beneath could hold bedding if you wish, or of course be clothed with ferns, the ideal accompaniment to early bulbs, and you'll then have a soft cool green outlook for the heat of a summer's day. True, you'll have less space for your 'roses round the door' but then in summer you'll most likely be 'down the garden' anyway, where evergreens will inevitably form the perfect backdrop to your roses and perennials, naturally.
There are exceptions: I wouldn't for example, be without the large Mahonia outside our living room window which manages to cast no shade and yet flowers for three months each winter. With the additional benefit that it draws in flocks of winter birds that somehow manage to feed on the flowers without seeming to spoil the display.

**

I have a friend who has variegated hollies and laurels planted in view of a window. Now these are not usually plants I like much, because I always feel that foliage colour is much more difficult to use in the garden than flower colour, since it seems to clash with other things much more easily; it's somehow much more strident than flower colour, and so much more 'there' all the time.
However, my friend has planted these under the shade of trees, a little distance from where they're usually viewed, so that they fade into the background in summer and are hardly noticed. But in winter when the leaves are gone from the trees, they suddenly shine out, all the better for being in the shelter and brightening this otherwise dull spot, so those at least are good winter evergreens.
Jasmine on the other hand, I'm in two minds about; on the one hand it does give a good display, and for a long time but I can't help but think that the common Winter Jasmine is better by far than the summer flowering forms. But in all other respects it's just such a boring little climber, it really is just such a 'sit on its own on a pew at the back of the church' kind of a plant. Not one that fits at all with the main idea, that maybe it's best to plant for the summer when you really can enjoy your garden most, and let the winter take care of itself.

Name Game

Many plants are not good naturalists and they neither know nor care anything for the differences between wilderness, farmland or garden. Why should they, when such classifications are only human inventions, and we often don't bother to mark the divisions between them with anything more than a strand of wire, which hardly presents any barrier at all to a healthy plant. Yet it's just those plants that often 'sit astride the fence' that I generally find to be the most fascinating of all.

Of course almost all of the divisions we see in seamless and unmapped nature are but flecks in the human eye, none more so than that which divides one gardener's scorned weed which leaps the fence uninvited, from a neighbour's rare wilding, difficult and shy, because of course in different soils they may well be just two faces of the same plant. And do we not all make mistakes sometimes? Charmed by a smiling face, we happily open the garden gate to a dangerous fifth columnist.

I have to live – perhaps forever – with the long-term consequences of the days when, with a large new garden to fill, I turned a blind eye to the Bloody Cranesbill; it is after all a pretty wild flower and only modest in stature. Yet even now, many years later, it still turns up in every odd corner it can find. Fortunately I acted more quickly and decisively with the wild Chicory, though I do still hope to find a safe and problem-free way of growing it because there can be few flowers that are so strikingly sky blue in colour.

Yet there are many more ambiguous plants I grow which in other soils, and in the eyes of no doubt more critical gardeners, would be seen as beyond the pale but which to me seem to give few problems relative to the pleasures their company brings. I would like to make a plea, for example, for the common field poppies which are I think very much misunderstood, for though they may well be a pernicious weed on arable land, poppies can in fact prove quite a challenge to grow in the garden. The poppy is, after all, the ultimate of opportunist annuals, a true pioneer species of disturbed ground, a real weed to the farmer if ever there was one and yet in the garden without the benefits of harvesting and ploughing, the little populations of deliberately sown plants can fade away quite rapidly, especially when faced with competition from deep rooted perennials. If you do find it too embarrassing to grow what many people regard as a weed, then you can try the Shirley hybrids which come in a

range of colours excluding the red, and thereby give a safe illusion of cultivation. The cultivated Iceland, Californian and Oriental poppies are all well known to be safe, presenting no danger to either your garden or your social position.
However, let me issue a caution regarding the Yellow Horned Welsh poppy: this is truly a very deep-rooted perennial which self seeds everywhere and resists control by both the spade and even a full can of weedkiller. Yet this is one of the most common poppies to find on sale!

**

There are quite a few other common weeds that I'm quite happy to tolerate a little of in the garden, such the Red Campion and also Honesty, both of which can go too far and overwhelm the plot if given too much freedom, but I merely keep their ambitions under control by waging a gentle war of attrition in the wilder corners of the garden, rather than aiming for total annihilation, and this seems to work well enough to keep both them and me happy.
With the Geums such as the wild Water-Avens, Geum rivale, I'm not so kind because the flowers, though interesting and sweet, seem a slightly dull reward for the price of putting up with the really annoying seeds which drill into your socks and trousers, causing real pain and no little discomfort. It would be bad enough if it wasn't for the fact that their foliage resembles so closely that of the cultivated Geums that it becomes hard work to distinguish them when weeding. The garden Geums, however, always seemed to me to be in complete contrast to the slightly dull wildings, a little gaudy and coarse, so I've long since solved the problem by getting rid of the garden types as well and just keeping a few Water-Avens by the pond.
The reverse happened with the Kingcup, Caltha palustris, for though I've always found it to make a fine problem-free garden plant, the wild type is perhaps a little too vigorous for a small garden pond. The cultivated double form, however, is much more modest in growth and easier to keep under control, which made me decide to keep it alone in my pond, banishing the wild form to the field drain on the outer edge of the garden. It's said that another advantage of the double garden form is that it keeps its flowers for longer than the wild plant but in truth I've not noticed much difference.
Of course whether you want a plant in the garden or not depends not just on your tastes but also on the time and place in which you

intend to plant it, and what you then want from it. Some plants undoubtedly have difficult habits but I'm fortunate in that there is a semi-wild stream which runs through the garden and the far bank isn't really a part of the tidy garden where precious plants are kept. I can therefore use this space to grow many of those things which, though I like them a lot, I wouldn't like to let them loose among valued plants in neat borders. (Actually none of my borders are neat but we'll let that pass for the sake of the argument.) The advantage of this is that I can enjoy growing things like Euphorbia robbiae and other invaders like Ransomes which help to control the weediness in a wild corner without me having to leap the stream too often. It's worth thinking about this since many people have rough isolated corners they can use this way, and which often just get neglected but would be much used if people realised what an asset they can be in this respect.

**

There are though plenty of plants which are surely equally valued whichever side of the fence they appear. Anyone who doesn't think, for example, that the common primrose is always a precious gift from nature whatever its situation, is not likely to take any joy from a garden, and so if there are such people they wouldn't wish to read about planting anyway. Since the Primula entered gardens many years ago it has given rise to a whole range of new types, in many colours and often with much larger flowers and sometimes an extended season. Yet even so, I can't help but find these cultivars a little disappointing – not that there's anything wrong with them, they're nearly all perfectly good plants – it's just that it seems to me that none of them quite withstands comparison with the common wild form.

The wild type seems more trouble free, healthier and brighter in colour; it also possesses a delicacy and a freedom from disease and blotches that the cultivars lack. However wonderful the breeders' skills are in producing so many different colours, I still can't find them as pleasing as that pure yellow and cream brightness of the wild form which seems to glow out of the hedge bottom saying, 'Now is spring beginning, but beware the season is as fragile as I am, yet be wise like me and venture little'. A set of properties that are true I think of many flowers when grown in their natural colour forms.

**

Sometimes (though I'm sure some people will think it perverse of me) I'm quite happy to reverse the normal trend in the garden and will even try my best to weed out garden plants in order to make space for weeds – well perhaps I would call them wild flowers. A case in point is the Creeping Jenny which, although listed as a garden flower, is regarded by many as perhaps a bit of a weed, mainly because of its generous spreading habit. Yet I think it a fine and pretty plant which carpets the ground with attractive evergreen leaves and pleasant flowers of a good bright strong yellow. Yet even so I too am trying to reduce its hold on the garden, not that I would mind if it carpeted the whole space, it's just that I'm trying to make more room for its close and fairly similar cousin, Yellow Pimpernel. The advantage of the Pimpernel is that, as well as being a rare wild flower which deserves help, it's also in many ways a much more refined plant than Creeping Jenny. This is because although, taking a casual glance the two seem similar in habit leaf and flower, when you look more carefully you soon see that the Pimpernel is altogether more stylish. The flowers are golden stars, more open and shapely than the more rounded goblets of Jenny, while the leaves are more delicate and finely pointed and the habit is less raggedy and coarse.

It's not just botanical names that can be confusing. The vernacular, or if you like, 'English' names can be just as bad. (I say 'English' in inverted commas because of course very few of them are truly Anglo-Saxon in origin, just as few of the botanical names are truly Latin.) For example I grow two forms of so-called Valerian in my garden which, save for the fact that both sometimes have clustered heads of pink flowers and both can be found growing wild, they couldn't really be more different, and are certainly not related.

The Red Valerian Centranthus ruber, although perhaps the more common and often seen growing wild in stony places as well as on walls, is not actually a native but comes from southern Europe. It's an attractive plant well worth some garden space, with shiny greyish leaves and bright pink pompom flowers carried at knee height; there are also some less common red and white forms which are equally attractive. It's a weed in some places, especially quarries, railway cuttings and the like but as long as you don't mind a little self seeding, it's rarely a big problem, though if you're organic and averse to weedkiller then you need to get the seedlings out quickly

because when established, the tap roots are strong and difficult to shift.
The so-called true Valerian, Valeriana officinalis, is a much bigger plant, growing to eye level in my garden. Much more impressive even though softer in colour, it's also a true native and prefers a richer, moister soil. It's never a problem in my garden, though I would think that in some places it could be a pest, being very generous with its airborne seeds, yet it's spectacular in its size and its soft hairy foliage with the looser pink flower heads makes it well worth a little bother.
Valeriana officinalis is the Valerian of medicine, being used to help with sleep and relaxation, though it should be used with caution because it's addictive and has some side effects. No doubt like many traditional herbal medicines it wouldn't be considered safe enough to market, had it been produced yesterday in a laboratory. Why however it should have given its name to a plant so different is hard to see, unless there was a shortage of letters in the alphabet at the time.

**

Such things often lead to confusion, especially among new gardeners; it was said that that's why it's better always to use the scientific, Linnaean, botanical or binominal names, as they're variously called, though having so many names just for the system doesn't exactly inspire confidence because the common, vernacular or English names vary so much from place to place. The trouble with that of course is that the scientific names also vary a lot, changing not with the geography but with time so that books written in different decades often use completely different names for the same plants. The common British native fern called the Hart's Tongue, for example, has had five changes of name at least in the last two centuries that I know of, and at least two of them still appear on labels.
So why not, you may think, just use Hart's Tongue as a name, at least that way, if you pick up a gardening book from the last century you'll know what it's talking about. There's some sense in that but it must be said that the scientific binominals are generally more accurate, and where they do change it's generally plainly recorded. The best thing that you can do in my limited experience, is to learn both because that way not only are you able to check one against

the other but also because you'll find that when once you begin to gain some knowledge, then the history of naming and the relationships between the names becomes an interesting subject in its own right. And if you doubt that, then I should tell you that I would be of all people the least likely to promote such a thing if it weren't true, being quite adverse to learning names and never having actively applied myself to the task at all, being content to have absorbed what little I know by osmosis as I went along.

I've never forgotten the wisdom of Richard Feynman when talking of bird watching, 'You can know the name of a bird in all the languages of the world but when you're finished, you know absolutely nothing whatever about the bird. So let's look at the bird and see what it's doing – that's what counts – I learned very early the difference between knowing the name of something and knowing something.'

Yet having said that sometimes names can charm and even tell you something about a plant's character. Sweet Cicely for example could hardly be a more pleasant sounding English name for native umbel Myrrhis odorata, and in fact the sweet, and the odorata part of the name does tell you something useful, for Cicely was a valued culinary herb in the past. Having a pleasant, slightly aniseed-type flavor, it was use to sweeten food, especially in the days before sugar was widely used or affordable. I also suspect, since it's not very 'sweet' in the modern sense of the word, it was most used in the days when the word sweet meant 'wholesome' or 'un-decayed' rather than sugary as it does today. That's all of little use to the gardener, however, who I suspect would far sooner know that in the garden it's a pleasant cow parsley-like flower with delicate white umbels held perhaps waist high at most, not spectacular but pleasing and with a slight tendency to sow itself about a bit more than is really wanted.

One wildflower I wouldn't be without in the garden, though, is the native Violet, or Viola odorata, another plant with the odorata minor name. Its English name may not tell you much about the plant itself but few plant names could be more richly entwined in human culture, giving us at the very least a name for both a class of scents and a range of colours.

I grow it mainly because it's one of the year's true seasonal markers. It grows in the woodland part of my garden, never having moved far from where it was planted, and each year it reappears just when you feel the need of a spring lift for your spirits. There aren't many of them and I don't need a lot, since half the joy of them is in finding just a scattered few poking through, much as you would in a wild hedge bank on a country walk. They grow quite happily without much need for thought or care on my part, coming up alongside some primroses and the two make an almost perfect colour combination. I think this is perhaps the best way to grow them, just plant them alongside some other modest plants in a quiet corner and leave them undisturbed.

**

While we're on the subject of plants with interesting names I'll probably grow the native Stitchwort in exactly the same way, when I manage to get hold of some. I don't have it yet but it's very much on my wish list, because to my mind it's one of our most beautiful wild flowers. You probably know it, even if you aren't familiar with wild flowers, since it's the very common white star-like flower never more than knee high that grows in many hedge bottoms and ditches. Its English name, which refers to its use in treating the 'stitch' and other forms of cramp, doesn't do it any favours since it would be hard to think of a prettier plant with a more ugly name. Much better is the Latin scientific name, Stellaria holostea, meaning 'little stars' which sums it up much better.

Also white in flower is the Woodruff, a lovely creeping carpeter, quite dense and useful for covering the ground and keeping out the weeds where nothing taller than knee high is wanted. The flowers are bright delicate clusters of small white daisies but it's perhaps best not to plant it beside really delicate plants as it's quite vigorous and will overwhelm small things if not controlled. Its other slight downside is the fact that the foliage, though much thicker and more attractive, does have a strong resemblance to that of cleavers, the horrible clinging little creeper with the felt-like leaves and seeds which stick to clothing and animals' fur, so that if the two become entangled it's hard to sort them out.

If you think, however, that you can have too much white and you'd like a ground cover plant (especially for a shady spot) which is, for example, blue in flower, then you couldn't do better than to choose another native wildflower, the Bugle, or Ajuga reptans. This colours the May garden with stout church spire-like spikes of blue flowers about 20cm high, and which grow on top of ground hugging shiny leaves. It can be bought in a number of cultivated forms, most of which have coloured leaves, often in shiny metallic shades of bronze copper or pewter grey. To my mind, and at least on my soils, it bring with it few problems and is one of those flowers you can just plant and admire.

Much the same can be said of the Wood Anemones, both the white Anemone nemorosa and the vibrantly blue A. blanda. Only the A. nemorosa is a true native but apart from the colour both are quite similar and equally hardy. They make a grand display in my woodland garden in the dull period before the ferns and summer flowers start to emerge. The sight of them always takes me back to the time when I was perhaps eleven or twelve years old, and I first saw a wood carpeted in their dazzling white stars. I couldn't at first believe that they could possibly be native wild flowers, and was sure they had to be some escaped exotic variety.

I only wish that the frequently red but often vibrantly pink A. coronaria of the Mediterranean was nearly as hardy, for the larger almost poppy-like flowers are well worth having, and annoyingly I know that it can be grown in some of the very mild areas of the British Isles but not of course here in the cold north east, and though I could plant some in a pot, a wildflower potted always seems as sad as a songbird caged.

Yet in my garden, these wildflowers of which I write are as free as in the wild, free to increase and spread if they wish – perhaps to fail its true sometimes – to persist down the years and delight future generations, or even to jump the fence and annoy the neighbours. But if my neighbours are good people they will surely value the gift, and if my neighbours have not the appreciation to value a wildflower for its beauty and wildness, and are lazy with their weeding as well, then a small annoyance is the best I can wish them.

Umbrellas

Some friends and their children joined me for a walk last year. It was high summer and I hadn't taken that particular route for several weeks, so hadn't thought just how much the plant life along the stream bank would have grown. This wasn't surprising really since it was never any real problem to me, not usually warranting a second thought. Children of course have a different perspective, and so all went well until we came to a point where the bank was now completely filled for a length of perhaps ten yards with a solid mass of stinging nettles. "That's no problem, I'll trample a path through them for you, so that you won't get stung." It was quickly and easily done and I soon returned, having cleared the path.
It didn't help of course, even nettles laid flat on the ground seem intimidating to small people, especially when there still remained banks of them, towering like the menacing fairy tale dark forests on either side. So I went back and forth several times making the path even wider but it was all pointless. No matter how wide the path or flat the nettles lying on the ground, the irrational fear of them was just too strong and no persuasion would convince them that it could possibly be safe. At last we were forced to give in to the democratic will and take a different way, which was no problem except for myself, since it involved leaving the trees and walking a long way in the sun; at least the children didn't have such a fear of the strong sun that those with very bald heads do.

**

Yet it's easy for anyone with even half a memory to understand the children's perspective; things look very different when you're young. Nettle stings bite more viciously when your skin is still thin and sensitive, and plants half ignored in adulthood are massive and imposing obstacles when you're of small stature and have a strictly limited geography.

Besides nettles there were, as I remember, several other plants which always seemed to dominate our world in our youth, such as the striking and bold Rosebay Willowherb or Fireweed – the Epilobum as it is known botanically. With its dense stands of tall stout stems and unforgettable bright red flowers, in early childhood it seemed huge and I suspect it's still one of that special canon of plants which every child knows. The other flowers that we all knew and which seemed to be everywhere in the outdoor spaces that children were then allowed to roam freely in, were the Umbellifers, those plants whose flowers come in flat sprays supported by many branching stems, superficially just like umbrellas – especially the common Cow Parsley, Anthriscus sylvestris of the hedgerow.

Partly this was because in those days it seemed to be a large and impressive plant – more than strong enough to be a real barrier to small people but yet not so much of one that you couldn't adventure a passage through it if you were determined enough so that it became a real jungle flower, holding you never knew how much adventure in its deep stands. The hollow stems, too, found many uses in custom and imagination, from real pea shooters to imagined pipes and flutes.

But there was more to it than that. I think that even then there seemed to be something exceptional about the plant's flowers – they were after all, quite close to face level through many of our more important formative years, and I also think that even quite young children are conscious of the fact that these flowers are completely different from what we were taught to perceive of as typical flowers. Give a child a brush and a pencil and ask for a flower, and nine times out of ten you'll get an open flower with petals on the outside, such as buttercup or a daisy. Hardly ever will you get a tubular flower like a honeysuckle or an umbel like the cow parsley.

Yet when we looked closely at our world we couldn't help but be aware of the structure of an umbel. It's perhaps the first flower most children notice that has a special structure to it, which sets it aside from all what we imagine to be most others. It follows then that the umbels, though we weren't conscious of it, must have played a small but profound role in our mindscapes at that time, just as they did in our landscapes.

But we grow older and more cynical with time. Even when we've passed the hiatus of willful adolescent self-obsession, that dulling still continues, so that the umbel of the hedgerow goes unnoticed except when it blocks the view, and the plant which offers so much to the birds and bees and the children, seems to us no more than an unnecessary ingredient in the hay. It's not surprising therefore, that of all our native plants it should be the common wild cow parsley that has inspired a popular folk tale, exactly about just that sad lack of vision we all have when it comes to valuing the truly familiar.

**

It appears that one alternate name for the plant is Queen Ann's Lace and it's said by some that the name refers to the wife of James 1 who was a skilled and famous lace maker. But there is another, perhaps much later story, about how the plant acquired this name, a story which has been repeated many times and appears in many different versions, few of which, I suspect, contain more than the slightest trace of literal truth.

Indeed, so complex is the tangled history of the anecdote that I can't tell you whether it should be described as a myth, fairy tale, legend or just an apocryphal literary invention, though the frequency of its reuse must testify to a valuable inner truth. So many are the versions that I make no apology for quoting this one just because I like it best.

It would seem that in some century past Britain was visited by the then queen of Denmark. During the visit the queen, known to be an enthusiastic gardener, was taken to see a number of England's better gardens, culminating in a particularly fine botanic garden that may have been Kew, Chelsea, or Chatsworth in Derbyshire, depending on who is relating the story.

She was, it appears, pleased and impressed by everything, and her pleasure in all that she saw charmed everyone. So that it being very near the end of her trip, and wishing to make a gracious gift, her hosts asked her which of all the many rare, strange, and exotic plants she would like to have potted and packed for her return to Denmark. This, of course represented an extremely expensive offer many years ago when plants still commanded very high prices. She replied that what she would really like most of all was, "Some of the wonderful white lace flower that grows in all the English hedgerows". The story is almost certainly apocryphal since the name Queen Ann's Lace for white umbels was already well established long before any of those fine gardens were planned. But it does make the important point about just how much we overlook the commonplace and fail to appreciate its wonderful and major contribution to our landscapes. What after all is a more significant element in our national myth than the country lane, and what would a country lane be without a gentle dusting of white summer snow blending the hedges with the verges into one whole wonderful composition?

**

The contribution of the umbels to the national diet and the vegetable garden however is certainly major, and this needs no argument from me. Just the short list of names that I can remember easily seems more than impressive enough: Carrot, Lovage, Celery, Coriander, Parsnip, Caraway, Parsley, Sweet Cicely, Dill, Celeriac, Aniseed, Cumin, Angelica, Fennel and Chervil. Not to mention the once popular Elizabethan sweetmeats Eringoes that were apparently in those far times made from the stewed and sweetened roots of the wild Eryngium maritimum or Sea Holly which seem now to have gone somewhat out of fashion. And in some ways that's perhaps no bad thing, since too many people harvesting the rare sea holly from the beaches could be a real threat to the species. Yet curiosity alone still makes you wonder about the lost taste of what was once a famous delicacy.

Yet despite that, the only the umbels which seem to have made it regularly into the ornamental garden are the sea hollies themselves, and the masterworts or Astrantia, neither of which has a typical umbel type of flower. In fact at a superficial glance both of them look much more like the closely related Compositae (daisies in other words) than the true umbels, while ironically the one group of plants which many people grow commonly in their gardens and perhaps often think of as umbels, namely the Achilleas or Yarrows, are in fact members of the Compositea.

You may think that this is just another example of the perversity of botanists, but if you can find or borrow a specimen of each and take them carefully to pieces, you'll see the logic of it for yourself (it's easier and less prickly to see it with the masterworts than the sea hollies). The flowers of the masterwort quite clearly spread out on little stems rather than being seated on a base like the typical daisy, and even if you don't get the botanical logic of it totally, you'll have a good excuse to spend a pleasant hour examining closely the structure of some beautiful flowers.

It would seem therefore that even when we grow the umbels we prefer that they should preferably not look like such. It's true that a couple of the families' members have a bad reputation for being highly toxic, and it's possible that all their relatives are then seen as being implicated. It's true that the poisonous umbels are often quite dangerous because they're apparently difficult for both humans and animals to tell apart from those that are safe to eat; the water-dropwort, for example, with its likeness to watercress makes it a moderate danger to the unwary, as does the poison of fool's parsley.

The really bad reputation, though, belongs of course to the hemlock, Conium maculatum, the tall powerfully-built umbel with the slightly sinister purple spots on its stems, which is famous as one of the traditional herbal poisons. Yet that may just be an historical memory of more dangerous times because it would be hard to imagine anyone finding hemlock and tucking into it by accident. The giant hogweed doesn't even need to be eaten, merely touching it can cause painful rashes and blisters on the skin, but it is perhaps the most sinister looking of all plants.

It should be pointed out, though, that poisons are really no more common in the umbels in general than they are in any other group of plants, while the umbels that are poisonous are so well documented that it's easy to avoid them. No, I suspect it's much more likely to be simply that the umbels are too richly associated with the semi-wilderness of uncultivated ground to be welcomed into our gardens, though we may admire them in the hedgerow beside a common country lane – and what could be more lovely than a common country lane, and how many of us manage to use our precious over-tended garden space to half such a good effect?

Yet do we not like there to be neat divisions and categories to our thinking; this plant to be admired in the wild and this one in the garden? Some plants could be likened to domestic spouses who help with the wallpaper hanging and the carpet laying, and some are wild lovers, admired precisely because they never will be domesticated – to be embraced only briefly, and all the more exciting because we know the embrace is ephemeral, only to be indulged on reckless sabbaticals far from home.

And yet I could still dearly wish that I had the space to make a border of umbels in the garden. It would perhaps have only a short season in high summer but just think of the spectacle, with tall Angelica and Giant Fennel at the back, leading down through Lovage, Bronze Fennel and Flowering Parsnip in the middle, to the Pink Cow Parsley and Sweet Cecily at the front.

The true proof that it is the wild associations of the umbels that exclude them from the garden must be that two of the most commonly domesticated of all the umbels – Chaerophyllum hirsutum 'Roseum', the rose chervil and Anthriscus sylvestris 'Ravenswing' – are quite strongly coloured forms, which could never be taken for anything that would grow in the wild, the first having very atypical pink flowers and the second dark almost black foliage. It is true, though, that both of them are good garden plants, well worth growing, though Ravenswing tends not to be very persistent in the long term and therefore requires more upkeep than I would care to give for just a colour novelty. Yet I cannot still help but think that when there are so many great umbels to be grown, it's merely what the Victorians would have called a 'deficiency of taste' that stops them being more widely grown.